MEAT

VERY LEAN MEAT AND SUBSTITUTES LIST

One exchange equals 0 grams carbohydrate, 7 grams protein, 0–1 grams fat, and 35 calories.

One very Lean Meat Exchange is equal to any one of the following items.

Cheese with 1 gram or less fat per ounce:

Fat-free cheese	1 oz.
Nonfat or low-fat cottage cheese	¼ cup

Fish: Fresh or frozen cod, flounder, haddock, halibut, trout; tuna (fresh or canned in water) — 1 oz.

Game: Buffalo, duck, or pheasant (no skin), ostrich, venison — 1 oz.

Poultry: Chicken or turkey (white meat, no skin), Cornish hen (no skin) — 1 oz.

Shellfish: Clams, crab, imitation shellfish, lobster, scallops, shrimp — 1 oz.

Other:

Egg substitutes, plain	¼ cup
Egg whites	2
Hot dogs with 1 gram or less fat per ounce*	1 oz.
Kidney (high in cholesterol)	1 oz.
Processed sandwich meats with 1 gram or less fat per ounce such as chipped beef,* deli thin shaved meats, turkey ham	1 oz.
Sausage with 1 gram or less fat per ounce	1 oz.

Count as 1 Very Lean Meat and 1 Starch Exchange

Dried beans, lentils, peas, (cooked)	½ cup

LEAN MEAT AND SUBSTITUTES LIST

One exchange equals 0 grams carbohydrate, 7 grams protein, 3 grams fat, and 55 calories.

One Lean Meat Exchange is equal to any one of the following items.

Beef: USDA Select or Choice grades of lean beef trimmed of fat, such as flank, round, and sirloin steak; ground round; roast (chuck, rib, rump); steak (cubed, porterhouse, T-bone); tenderloin — 1 oz.

Cheese:

Cheeses with 3 grams or less fat per ounce	1 oz.
4.5% fat cottage cheese	¼ cup
Grated Parmesan	2 Tbsp.

Fish:

Herring (uncreamed or smoked)	1 oz.
Oysters	6 medium
Salmon (fresh or canned), catfish	1 oz.
Sardines (canned)	2 medium
Tuna (canned in oil, drained)	1 oz.

Game: Goose (no skin), rabbit — 1 oz.

Lamb: Chop, leg, roast — 1 oz.

Pork: Lean pork, such as boiled, canned, or cured ham; Canadian-style bacon*; center loin chop; fresh ham; tenderloin — 1 oz.

Poultry: Chicken and turkey (dark meat, no skin), chicken white meat (with skin), domestic duck or goose (well-drained of fat, no skin) — 1 oz.

Veal: Lean chop, roast — 1 oz.

Other:

Hot dogs with 3 grams or less fat per ounce*	1½ oz.
Liver, heart (high in cholesterol)	1 oz.
Processed sandwich meat with 3 grams or less fat per ounce such as kielbasa or turkey pastrami	1 oz.

MEDIUM-FAT MEAT AND SUBSTITUTES LIST

One exchange equals 0 grams carbohydrate, 7 grams protein, 5 grams fat, and 75 calories.

One Medium-Fat Meat Exchange is equal to any one of the following items.

Beef: Most beef products fall into this category (corned beef; ground beef; meatloaf; Prime grades of meat trimmed of fat, such as prime rib; short ribs) — 1 oz.

Cheese: With 5 grams or less fat per ounce

Feta	1 oz.
Mozzarella	1 oz.
Ricotta	2 oz. (¼ cup)

Fish: Any fried fish product — 1 oz.

Lamb: Ground, rib roast — 1 oz.

Pork: Boston butt, chop, cutlet, top loin — 1 oz.

Poultry: Chicken dark meat (with skin), fried chicken (with skin), ground turkey or ground chicken — 1 oz.

Veal: Cutlet (cubed or ground, unbreaded) — 1 oz.

Other:

Egg (high in cholesterol, limit to 3 per week)	1
Sausage with 5 grams or less fat per ounce	1 oz.
Soy milk	1 cup
Tofu	4 oz. (½ cup)

HIGH-FAT MEAT AND SUBSTITUTES

One exchange equals 0 grams carbohydrate, 7 grams protein, 8 grams fat, and 100 calories.

These items are high in saturated fat, cholesterol, and calories and may raise blood cholesterol levels if eaten regularly. One High-Fat Meat Exchange is equal to any one of the following items.

Cheese: All regular cheeses, such as American,* cheddar, Monterey Jack, Swiss — 1 oz.

Pork: Ground pork, pork sausage, spareribs — 1 oz.

Other:

Bacon	3 slices (20 slices/lb.)
Hot dog (chicken or turkey)*	1 (10/lb.)
Processed sandwich meats with 8 grams or less fat per ounce, such as bologna, pimiento loaf, salami	1 oz.
Sausage, such as bratwurst, Italian, knockwurst, Polish, smoked	1 oz.

Count as 1 High-Fat Meat plus 1 Fat Exchange.

Hot dog (beef, pork, or combination)*	1 (10/lb.)
Peanut butter (contains unsaturated fat)	2 Tbsp.

* = 400 mg or more sodium per exchange

VEGETABLE

One Vegetable Exchange equals 5 grams carbohydrate, 2 grams protein, 0 grams fat, and 25 calories.

One Vegetable Exchange is equal to ½ cup cooked vegetable or vegetable juice or 1 cup raw vegetable of the following.

Artichoke
Artichoke hearts
Asparagus
Beans (green, Italian, wax)
Bean sprouts
Beets
Broccoli
Brussels sprouts
Cabbage
Carrots
Cauliflower
Celery
Cucumber
Eggplant
Green onions or scallions
Greens (collard, kale, mustard, turnip)
Kohlrabi
Leeks
Mixed vegetables (without corn, peas, or pasta)
Mushrooms
Okra
Onions
Pea pods
Peppers (all varieties)
Radishes
Salad greens (endive, escarole, lettuce, romaine)
Sauerkraut*
Spinach
Summer squash
Tomato
Tomatoes, canned
Tomato sauce*
Tomato/vegetable juice*
Turnips
Water chestnuts
Watercress
Zucchini

* = 400 mg or more sodium per exchange

COMMON MEASUREMENTS

3 teaspoons	= 1 tablespoon
4 tablespoons	= ¼ cup
5⅓ tablespoons	= ⅓ cup
4 ounces	= ½ cup
8 ounces	= 1 cup
1 cup	= ½ pint

The Food Exchanges continue on the inside back cover.

Better Homes and Gardens® Books
An imprint of Meredith® Books

Eat & Stay Slim
Editor: Kristi M. Fuller, R.D.
Contributing Editors: Diane Quagliani, R.D.; Marcia K. Stanley, R.D.;
    Mary Major Williams; Spectrum Communication Services
Associate Art Director: Tom Wegner
Copy Chief: Angela K. Renkoski
Test Kitchen Director: Sharon Stilwell
Test Kitchen Product Supervisor: Colleen Weeden
Photographer: Andy Lyons
Food Stylists: Lynn Blanchard, Dianna Nolin
Electronic Production Coordinator: Paula Forest
Editorial and Design Assistants: Judy Bailey, Jennifer Norris, Karen Schirm
Production Manager: Douglas M. Johnston
Prepress Coordinator: Marjorie J. Schenkelberg

Meredith® Books
Editor in Chief: James D. Blume
Managing Editor: Christopher Cavanaugh
Director, New Product Development: Ray Wolf
Vice President, General Manager: Jamie L. Martin

Better Homes and Gardens® Magazine
Editor in Chief: Jean LemMon
Executive Food Editor: Nancy Byal

Meredith Publishing Group
President, Publishing Group: Christopher M. Little
Vice President and Publishing Director: John P. Loughlin

Meredith Corporation
Chairman and Chief Executive Officer: Jack D. Rehm
President and Chief Operating Officer: William T. Kerr
Chairman of the Executive Committee: E.T. Meredith III

On the cover: Chicken Teriyaki with Summer Fruit, recipe on page 32
On page 3: Chicken with Mushroom Sauce, recipe on page 36

Our seal assures you that every recipe in *Eat & Stay Slim*
has been tested in the Better Homes and Gardens® Test Kitchen.
This means that each recipe is practical and reliable, and meets
our high standards of taste appeal. We guarantee your satisfaction
with this book for as long as you own it.

CONTENTS

INTRODUCTION

*A*chieving and maintaining a healthful weight offers many long-lasting benefits. You'll look and feel better day to day and reduce your risk of weight-related health problems as you get older.

But have you tried to lose weight in the past without lasting success? Perhaps you followed the latest weight-loss diet until you dropped a few pounds, but when you went off the diet—and returned to your old eating habits—the pounds came right back on.

Well, cross the word "diet" off your list. *Eat & Stay Slim* can help you adopt a healthful way of eating that you'll enjoy both as the pounds come off and once you reach your goal.

The information on the following pages will help you set a healthful goal weight, determine how many calories you need to safely lose weight, and show you how to develop new eating and activity habits that suit your lifestyle—so you can stay slim for a lifetime.

HOW LOW SHOULD YOU GO? SETTING A GOAL WEIGHT

The most healthful weight for you depends on many factors—your age, sex, height, and frame size, for instance. Also important is your body shape and where you carry extra fat. If you're more apple-shaped and carry extra fat on your abdomen, chances are you're at greater risk for developing health problems such as high blood pressure, heart disease, diabetes, and some cancers. If you're more pear-shaped and carry extra fat on your hips, buttocks, and thighs, extra pounds may not pose as much risk for you of these diseases.

The chart at *right* can help you determine whether you need to lose weight and, if so, the most healthful goal weight for you. If you are muscular or big-boned, a weight at the high end of your range may be best for you; if you don't have much muscle or are small-boned, a weight at the low end may be best.

When setting a goal weight, keep this thought in mind: Be reasonable. For permanent success, set your sights on a healthful, sensible weight that you can comfortably maintain, not a weight that is unrealistically low.

Be reasonable, too, in how quickly you expect to lose the excess weight. Nutrition experts say losing one-half to 1 pound a week at the most is the safest, most effective way to take off pounds. If you need help setting weight-loss goals, ask your doctor or a registered dietitian for advice or assistance.

WEIGHT CHART
Healthy weight ranges for men and women

Height	Pounds
4'10"	91-119
4'11"	94-124
5'0'"	97-128
5'1"	101-132
5'2"	104-137
5'3"	107-141
5'4"	111-146
5'5"	114-150
5'6"	118-155
5'7"	121-160
5'8"	125-164
5'9"	129-169
5'10"	132-174
5'11"	136-179
6'0"	140-184
6'1"	144-189
6'2"	148-195
6'3"	152-200
6'4"	156-205
6'5"	160-211
6'6"	164-216

Height is without shoes; weight without clothes

Source: Report of the Dietary Guidelines Advisory Committee on the Dietary Guidelines for Americans, 1995.

Pictured clockwise from top left: Spinach Soufflé in Cornmeal Crepes, page 68; Mixed Greens and Fruit Salad, page 75; Chocolate-Banana Shake, page 105, and Peach Smoothie, page 104; and Nutmeg-Apricot Rolls, page 19.

TEN STEPS TO SUCCESS

Note: If you have diabetes and want to incorporate the recipes in this book into your meal planning, contact your doctor or dietitian for assistance.

1. Look at the long and short of it. Establish short-term weight goals as well as a long-term goal. You'll feel good tracking your progress and reaching one weight-loss goal after another.

2. Celebrate your successes. Reward each success, but not with food. Instead, buy yourself a bouquet of flowers, treat yourself to a new pair of walking shoes, or go to a movie when you reach a short-term goal. Treat yourself to a new outfit or a complete makeover when you reach your long-term goal.

3. Keep a journal. A journal not only helps you track your weight-loss progress, but is a great place to monitor your feelings, plan eating strategies for special occasions, and even log-in compliments you receive as you lose weight.

4. Be patient. Some weeks you may not lose an ounce even though you're following your Daily Meal Plans to the letter. This could be due to your body adjusting to a lower calorie level or a change in your body's fluid balance. Stick with your plan, stay physically active, and over time your weight will come down.

5. Get label savvy. Read food labels to learn how foods fit into your Daily Meal Plans. Take special note of serving sizes and the amount of calories and fat in each serving. Look, too, for the food exchange information included on some packaged foods.

6. Plan. If you're attending a big birthday bash or going out for a special meal, work in some extra physical activity and bank some of your fat exchanges for a few days before and after. That way, you can splurge a little at the event.

7. Enjoy favorite foods. Who wants to give up foods they like? You can follow your Daily Meal Plans for a lifetime because they're flexible enough to let you include an occasional favorite and still lose or maintain your weight.

8. Expect setbacks. Nobody is perfect. If you slip off your plan, don't worry about it. An occasional slip-up doesn't make a difference in the grand scheme of things. Just get back on track as soon as possible.

9. Make it a family affair. Enlist your friends, mate, or children as cheerleaders in your slim-down effort. Ask them to choose recipes from this book that everyone will enjoy.

10. Seek support. A registered dietitian can give you support and advice on setting a weight goal, using the Food Exchange Lists, and choosing foods wisely. To find a registered dietitian in your area, call The American Dietetic Association at 800/366-1655.

CALORIE MATH: FIGURING YOUR DAILY NEEDS

How many calories do you need each day to reach your weight goal? It's easy to figure once you know a little calorie math.

A pound of body fat contains about 3,500 calories (about the same number as in a pound of butter or margarine). Figure the calorie math this way: If you eat 3,500 fewer calories than your body uses, you will shed 1 pound. So, if you take in 7,000 fewer calories, you will lose 2 pounds (of course, this is over a period of time).

How does this translate into everyday living? By eating 500 fewer calories than you burn up each day, you should lose about 1 pound a week. Or, cut only 250 calories each day and lose one-half pound per week. You can create this calorie deficit by consuming fewer calories, burning calories through physical activity, or, best yet, doing both. But it's in your own best interest not to cut calories severely. We don't recommend consuming less than 1,200 calories per day without the supervision of a doctor.

Here's an easy formula to help you estimate your daily calorie needs. Most moderately active people need to consume about 15 calories per pound to maintain weight. So, if you're a 133-pound woman, you need 15 calories times 133, or 1,995 calories per day for your weight to stay the same. To lose 1 pound in a week, you must achieve a calorie deficit of 500 calories per day. You can do this in several ways. For example, each day you could eat 400 fewer calories and burn off 100 extra calories with physical activity, or eat 300 fewer calories and burn off 200 extra calories. Whatever the combination, the choice is yours.

1,995	maintenance calories per day
-500	calories per day
1,495	calories per day to lose 1 pound per week

(If this example fits you, use the 1,500-calorie Daily Meal Plan on page 13 and the 1,500-calorie menu suggestions on pages 107 and 108.)

BEING ACTIVE: THE OTHER HALF OF THE WEIGHT-LOSS EQUATION

To win at weight loss, burning calories by being active is just as important as adopting a healthful eating plan. Health experts agree that totaling at least 30 minutes of moderate physical activity on most—and preferably all—days is a formula for success. The good news is you don't have to huff and puff at the gym to benefit. You can accumulate your "daily 30" in 10-minute chunks of activity throughout the day, though this won't burn as much fat as a full 30-minute session. The list below shows how long it takes to burn 100 calories by combining activities.

Activity	Minutes to Burn 100 Calories*
Aerobic dancing	14
Bicycling (10 mph)	14
Bicycling, stationary, moderate pace	12
Brisk walking (3.5 mph)	21
Gardening	17
Golf, pulling clubs	17
Roller blading	12
Running (6 mph)	8.5
Ski machine	9
Swimming laps	10.5

* Based on a 150-pound person

Numbers derived from "Compendium of Physical Activities: Classification of Energy Costs of Human Physical Activities" by Barbara E. Ainsworth, et al. in Medicine and Science in Sports and Exercise, 1993.

MAKE A PLAN

Once you determine the number of daily calories you need to reach your weight goal, choose the Daily Meal Plan and menus that are right for you. We've provided plans (page 13) and menus suggestions (pages 107 and 108) for 1,200, 1,500, 1,800, and 2,000 calories per day so you can lose then maintain your weight. The suggested menus include recipes from this book.

Use the blank meal plan on page 109 to record your own personal meal plan. Carry a photocopy of Your Meal Plan with you to work and restaurants.

Consider Your Meal Plan a blueprint for a lifetime of healthful and enjoyable eating. Each of the plans offers the following features.

■ **Built-in Good Nutrition:** Health experts recommend eating a diet high in carbohydrate, moderate in protein, and low in fat. Each plan provides about 55 percent of total daily calories from carbohydrate, 15 percent calories from protein, and 30 percent calories from fat. They also provide the right mix of grains, fruits, vegetables, meat, and dairy products to make sure you get all the daily nutrients you need.

■ **Freedom from Calorie-Counting:** Our Daily Menu Plans do all the work for you. Just eat the suggested number of Food Exchanges for your calorie level by choosing from the recipes in this book (which all have the exchanges clearly listed next to them). Supplement your recipe selections by choosing foods in each of the Food Exchange Lists (see inside covers of back and front of book for exchange lists and pages 107 and 108 for menu suggestions).

■ **Flexibility:** Because the menus, Daily Meal Plans, and Food Exchange Lists are designed to suit your tastes and lifestyle, you'll learn how to include favorite treats and on-the-go food choices, too.

GETTING TO KNOW THE FOOD EXCHANGE LISTS

One serving of a food is called an "exchange," because you can swap it for a serving of any other food or beverage on a particular list. For example, from the Starch List, you could exchange ⅓ cup of cooked brown rice for a small baked potato.

Foods are divided into six Basic Exchange Lists, a Free Foods List, a Special Foods List, and a Combination Foods List (see inside covers of back and front of book and the explanations on the next few pages). The foods on each Basic Exchange List contain about the same number of calories and amounts of carbohydrate, protein, and fat. The Free Foods List shows foods that contain few calories when eaten in the amounts indicated. The Special Foods List gives exchanges for foods that contain sugars or fat. The Combination Foods List gives exchanges for mixtures of food.

Using exchanges is easy once you learn the basics. Check each list for specific serving sizes.

THE FOOD EXCHANGE LISTS

STARCH LIST

Foods on the Starch List range from animal crackers to yams. One serving of foods from this list (bread, cereals, grains, pasta, starchy vegetables, crackers, snacks, and cooked dried beans, peas, and lentils) has about 80 calories, 15 grams of carbohydrate, 3 grams of protein, and a trace amount of fat. Most foods from the Starch List provide B vitamins and iron.

Although serving sizes vary, use the following guidelines for unlisted foods. (See more extensive lists for all food groups on the inside covers of front and back of book.)

ONE STARCH EXCHANGE IS:

1 OUNCE OF A BREAD PRODUCT, SUCH AS 1 SLICE OF BREAD
½ CUP OF COOKED CEREAL, GRAIN, PASTA, OR STARCHY VEGETABLE, SUCH AS CORN
¾ TO 1 OUNCE OF MOST SNACK FOODS

STARCH EXCHANGE TIPS

■ Most often, choose starches made with little or no added fat.
■ One serving of starchy vegetables (such as corn, potatoes, and peas) that is made with fat counts as 1 Starch Exchange and 1 Fat Exchange.
■ Use the "Starchy Foods Prepared with Fat" section of the Starch List to select foods such as French-fried potatoes, microwave popcorn, and muffins. A serving of these foods counts as 1 Starch Exchange and 1 Fat Exchange.
■ One serving of dried beans, peas, and lentils counts as 1 Starch Exchange and 1 Very Lean Meat Exchange.
■ Whole grains and dried beans, peas, and lentils are good sources of fiber.

MEAT AND MEAT SUBSTITUTES LIST

Meat, poultry, fish, eggs, cheese, peanut butter, and tofu belong on the Meat and Meat Substitutes List because they are excellent sources of protein, B vitamins, iron, and zinc. Because the fat and calorie content of meat products varies, the exchanges on this list are divided into the four groups shown below.

	Carbo. (grams)	Protein (grams)	Fat (grams)	Calories
Very lean	0	7	0-1	35
Lean	0	7	3	55
Medium-fat	0	7	5	75
High-fat	0	7	8	100

ONE MEAT EXCHANGE IS:

1 OUNCE COOKED MEAT, POULTRY, OR FISH
1 OUNCE CHEESE
1 EGG
½ CUP COOKED DRIED BEANS, PEAS, LENTILS
2 TABLESPOONS PEANUT BUTTER
3 SLICES BACON

MEAT EXCHANGE TIPS

■ The Daily Meal Plans and menus are written for medium-fat exchanges. Count a High-Fat Meat Exchange as 1 Meat Exchange plus ½ Fat Exchange.
■ One ounce of cooked lean meat, poultry, or fish is about the size of a small matchbox.
■ Think lean when selecting foods from this list. Choose cuts of meat with the words "round" or "loin" in the name (for example, ground round or pork tenderloin), skinless poultry, fish, and dry beans, peas, and lentils.
■ An exchange of dried beans, peas, or lentils counts as 1 Very Lean Meat Exchange and 1 Starch Exchange.
■ An exchange of peanut butter or a hot dog counts as 1 High-Fat Meat Exchange and 1 Fat Exchange.
■ Smaller serving sizes of peanut butter and bacon are counted as Fat Exchanges instead of Meat Exchanges (see Fat List).

VEGETABLE LIST

Enjoy vegetables often because they're low in calories and fat, and bursting with vitamins A and C, folic acid, iron, magnesium, and fiber. One Vegetable Exchange contains about 5 grams of carbohydrate, 2 grams of protein, 25 calories, and 1 to 4 grams of fiber.

ONE VEGETABLE EXCHANGE IS:

1 CUP OF RAW VEGETABLES SUCH AS LETTUCE, SPINACH, OR BROCCOLI FLOWERETS
½ CUP OF COOKED VEGETABLES OR VEGETABLE JUICE

VEGETABLE EXCHANGE TIPS

■ Several times weekly choose dark green, leafy vegetables (such as spinach, romaine lettuce, broccoli, and cabbage) and deep yellow and orange varieties (such as carrots and red peppers). Sweet potatoes and acorn squash are on the Starch List.
■ Good choices for vitamin C include tomatoes, peppers, greens, broccoli, cauliflower, and Brussels sprouts.
■ Select frozen vegetables made without butter or sauces.
■ Reduce the salt content of canned vegetables by draining, then rinsing them with tap water.

FRUIT LIST

Fruit is the perfect snack or dessert when you're in the mood for something sweet. Fruit gives you vitamins A and C, potassium, and fiber, all wrapped up in a handy, fat-free package. One Fruit Exchange supplies about 60 calories and 15 grams of carbohydrate. The Fruit List includes fresh, frozen, canned, and dried fruits, as well as fruit juices.

MOST FRUIT EXCHANGES EQUAL:

1 SMALL TO MEDIUM PIECE OF FRESH FRUIT, SUCH AS AN APPLE OR ORANGE
½ CUP OF CANNED OR FRESH FRUIT OR FRUIT JUICE
¼ CUP OF DRIED FRUIT

FRUIT EXCHANGE TIPS

■ Select deep yellow or orange fruits (cantaloupe, apricots, peaches, or mangoes) and "high C" options (oranges, grapefruits, strawberries, or kiwifruit).
■ Shave calories by choosing canned fruit packed in water, juice, or extra-light syrup.
■ Boost fiber by opting for whole fruit more often than juice.

MILK LIST

Milk and yogurt are excellent sources of calcium, the nutrient you need for strong, healthy bones. Milk products also provide protein, phosphorous, magnesium, and vitamins A, D, B_{12}, and riboflavin. Because the fat and calorie content of milk products varies, the exchanges on this list are divided into the three groups shown below.

	Carbo. (grams)	Protein (grams)	Fat (grams)	Calories
Skim/very low-fat	12	8	0-3	90
Low-fat	12	8	5	120
Whole	12	8	8	150

ONE MILK EXCHANGE IS:

1 CUP OF MILK
1 CUP OF YOGURT

MILK EXCHANGE TIPS

■ The Daily Meal Plans and menus are written for skim and very low-fat milk products. Count low-fat products as 1 Milk Exchange plus 1 Fat Exchange; count whole milk products as 1 Milk Exchange plus 1½ Fat Exchanges.
■ To keep calories, fat, and saturated fat at a minimum, select from the "Skim/Very Low-Fat" group most often.
■ You'll find chocolate milk, low-fat yogurt with fruit, ice cream, and frozen yogurt on the Special Foods List.

FAT LIST

Fat is a fooler: It packs a big calorie punch in a small package. Often hidden in foods, calorie-dense fats can add extra pounds quickly if you aren't careful. Eating too much fat—especially saturated fat—also can increase your risk for heart disease, diabetes, and some types of cancers. Each Fat Exchange provides about 5 grams of fat and 45 calories.

ONE FAT EXCHANGE IS:

1 TEASPOON VEGETABLE OIL, REGULAR MARGARINE, BUTTER, OR MAYONNAISE
1 TABLESPOON REGULAR SALAD DRESSING
6 ALMONDS OR CASHEWS, OR 4 PECAN OR WALNUT HALVES
2 TEASPOONS PEANUT BUTTER
1 SLICE BACON

FAT EXCHANGE TIPS
■ Foods on the Fat List are divided into unsaturated (monounsaturated and polyunsaturated) and saturated fats. Spend your Fat Exchanges on unsaturated fats most often.
■ Measure Fat List foods carefully to avoid extra calories.
■ Avocados, olives, and coconuts are on the Fat List.
■ Cream, half-and-half, and cream cheese also are on this list.
■ Larger serving sizes of peanut butter and bacon are counted as High-Fat Meat Exchanges instead of Fat Exchanges (see Meat List).

THE FREE FOODS LIST

Some things in life *are* free. The Free Foods List contains dozens of foods and drinks that contain less than 20 calories per serving. Feel free to enjoy up to three daily servings of the Free Foods listed with a serving size—no need to count them as exchanges. Eat all you'd like of the foods listed without a serving size.

THE SPECIAL FOODS LIST

Can you enjoy favorite goodies and still lose or maintain your weight? Absolutely! The Special Foods List helps you fit occasional sweet treats such as cakes, cookies, ice cream, and pie, as well as higher-fat snacks, such as potato chips and tortilla chips, into your Daily Meal Plan. Eat foods from this list in moderation.

SPECIAL FOODS EXCHANGE TIPS
■ Foods on this list are not as nutrient-dense as foods on the Starch, Fruit, or Milk lists. Moderation and balance are watchwords when choosing from this list.
■ Carefully note the serving sizes for the foods on this list. Because they generally contain added sugars or fat, serving sizes are often quite small.
■ Some choices count as one or more exchanges. Adjust your Daily Meal Plan accordingly.

COMBINATION FOODS LIST

"Mixed" foods such as casseroles, soups, pizza, and many of the recipes from this book, combine foods from two or more of the Food Exchange Lists. For the recipes in this book, Food Exchanges are calculated for you and appear with each recipe.

You will find exchanges for several mixed foods on the Combination Foods List. Many food manufacturers list exchanges on packages.

For foods that are not on the Food Exchange Lists or for your own recipes, estimate exchanges by determining what portion of an exchange each ingredient represents. For example, a serving of stew may contain 2 ounces of cooked lean beef (2 Lean Meat Exchanges), ½ cup of potato (1 Starch Exchange), and ½ cup of carrots (1 Vegetable Exchange).

FAST FOODS

You don't have to give up the convenience of fast foods while losing weight. When you're eating on the run, you can occasionally include fast food items in your meal planning. Follow these tips when choosing fast foods:

FAST FOOD TIPS
- Many fast food restaurants provide exchanges and other nutrition information about their menu items. Ask for it.
- To minimize calories and fat, choose fast foods such as grilled chicken sandwiches and smaller burgers more often.
- Practice portion control. Order the small bag of French fries or split them with a friend.
- Some fast food restaurants offer plain baked potatoes and salads with reduced- or low-calorie dressing.

USING RECIPES AND FOOD EXCHANGES IN YOUR DAILY MEAL PLAN

Your Daily Meal Plan shows your daily allotment of exchanges from each Food Exchange List. Eating the right amount of food is essential in order to keep your calories in line. For this reason, the recipes give a specific number of servings, and the Food Exchange Lists (see inside covers of back and front of book) define a specific amount of food for each exchange. Serving sizes differ within each list.

Most recipes in this book include exchanges from two or more groups. To make meal planning easy, the exchanges for a serving appear with each recipe. After choosing a recipe, subtract the exchanges for 1 serving from the total listed for the meal in your Daily Meal Plan. Select items from the Food Exchange Lists for the remaining exchanges.

MEAL PLANNING STEP-BY-STEP

Meal planning is a snap when you follow these seven easy steps:

1. Begin each meal with a main dish that is within your exchange guidelines for the meal. It might be just meat, poultry, or fish, or a recipe from this book. If you choose 3 ounces of broiled fish, mark off 3 Lean Meat Exchanges. Or, use 3 Medium-Fat Exchanges plus 1 Vegetable Exchange for a combination dish.
2. If you have 2 Starch Exchanges in your meal, you could choose 1 slice of bread and ⅓ cup of rice. Check off 2 Starch Exchanges.
3. You may choose a Fruit Exchange as a side dish or dessert. If so, mark it off.
4. How many Vegetable Exchanges do you have? If you have 2, you might choose ½ cup of green beans and a large broiled tomato.
5. Add 1 Milk Exchange if you plan to drink a glass of milk with your meal, or you can use it in cooking (for example, in a cream soup).
6. Determine any Fat Exchanges not used in cooking. One teaspoon of margarine used on the slice of bread equals 1 Fat Exchange.
7. Add Free Foods as desired. Coffee or tea might accompany the dessert.

SAFEGUARDING THE NEW, SLIMMER YOU

Congratulations! You've reached your goal weight and healthful eating and activity habits are second nature. Now that you've met your goal, you can enjoy more calories each day to maintain, rather than continue to lose, weight.

But, how can you make sure you'll stay slim? Continue to use one of the Daily Meal Plans (page 13), the Exchange Lists, and Your Meal Plan (page 109) to guide your food choices.

Here's how:

■ Calculate the number of daily calories you need to maintain your new weight. Remember, if you're moderately active, you need about 15 calories per pound. If your new weight is 125 pounds, you need about 1,875 calories per day to keep your weight the same.

■ Now choose a Daily Meal Plan that is slightly less than or equal to the number of calories you need for maintenance. If your goal is 1,875 calories, follow the 1,800-calorie plan.

■ If your calorie goal is more than the number of calories in the Daily Meal Plan you choose, add Food Exchanges to the plan to equal your

MORE TIPS ON USING YOUR DAILY MEAL PLAN AND FOOD EXCHANGE LISTS

■ To hit your calorie target, simply eat the total number of exchanges from each Basic Exchange List shown on your Daily Meal Plan.

■ For top nutrition, always eat the minimum number of exchanges shown from each Basic Exchange List.

■ Variety is the spice of life, so keep your Daily Meal Plan enjoyable by choosing a wide variety of foods from each Exchange List.

■ Each Daily Meal Plan provides for three meals plus two snacks a day. You also may divide your Food Exchanges into several mini meals.

■ It's OK to skip an exchange or two at any meal. Just move it to another meal or enjoy it as a snack later in the day.

■ If you add an exchange to a meal or wish to include one as a snack, subtract this exchange from another meal that day.

■ Start out by measuring Food Exchanges carefully. Then you can estimate serving sizes both at home and when dining out.

■ To simplify counting exchanges, grocery shopping, and cooking, plan meals for an entire day or several days at once.

■ Remember, you can exchange foods on a list to your heart's content, but don't exchange between lists. (One exception: You may occasionally trade a Starch, Milk, or Fruit Exchange for an exchange from the Special Foods List.)

■ Beware of alcohol. It provides calories but no nutrients. Alcoholic drinks are not included on any of the Exchange Lists, so if you have a drink, it will put you over your calorie limit for the day. One jigger (1½ ounces) of 90-proof liquor supplies about 110 calories. Eight ounces of beer provides 114 calories; light beer has slightly less. Dry table wine has about 87 calories per 3½ ounces.

target. For example, if your target calorie total is 1,875 calories, add 75 calories in Food Exchanges to the 1,800-calorie plan. Or, increase your serving size to make up the difference. The chart *below* lists the calorie values of an exchange in each Exchange List.

■ When you add extra exchanges, choose nutrient-dense foods most often. For example, 1 ounce of mozzarella cheese, a Medium-Fat Meat Exchange, added to your sandwich gives you an extra 75 calories—and is a good source of calcium, too.

■ If your calorie goal is much higher—perhaps 2,400 calories (the number of calories to maintain the weight of a 160-pound, moderately active man)—follow the 2,000-calorie plan. Then add servings from a variety of the Exchange Lists.

■ Don't forget the power of physical activity. Thirty minutes of daily activity will help you stay slim—and healthy, too.

CALORIE VALUES FOR FOOD EXCHANGE LISTS

Use this chart if you need to add exchanges to your Daily Meal Plan. Add enough exchanges to equal the calories in your daily calorie target.

Basic Exchange (1)	Calories
Starch	80
Meat and Meat Substitutes	
Very lean	35
Lean	55
Medium-fat	75
High-fat	100
Vegetable	25
Fruit	60
Milk	
Skim/very low-fat	90
Low-fat	120
Whole	150
Fat	45

DAILY MEAL PLANS

1,200 CALORIES

	Breakfast	Lunch	Snack	Dinner	Snack
STARCH (6)	1	2	1	1	1
MEAT (3)		1		2	
VEGETABLE (3)		1		1	1
FRUIT (2)	1			1	
MILK (Skim)(2)	½	1		½	
FAT (3)	1	1		1	

1,500 CALORIES

	Breakfast	Lunch	Snack	Dinner	Snack
STARCH (8)	2	2	1	2	1
MEAT (4)		1		3	
VEGETABLE (3)		1	1	1	
FRUIT (3)	1	1			1
MILK (Skim)(2)	½	½		1	
FAT (4)		1		2	1

1,800 CALORIES

	Breakfast	Lunch	Snack	Dinner	Snack
STARCH (9)	2	2	2	2	1
MEAT (4)		1		3	
VEGETABLE (3)		1		1	1
FRUIT (5)	1	1	1	1	1
MILK (Skim)(2)		1		1	
FAT (6)	2	2		2	

2,000 CALORIES

	Breakfast	Lunch	Snack	Dinner	Snack
STARCH (10)	2	2	2	2	2
MEAT (5)		2		3	
VEGETABLE (3)		1		2	
FRUIT (5)	2	1	1		1
MILK (Skim)(2)	1		1		
FAT (7)	1	2	1	2	1

Note: Totals for each group can be distributed among your meals and snacks however you choose. Meat Exchanges are based on medium-fat choices, assuming you'll choose a variety of meats that will average out to the midrange.

BREAKFAST

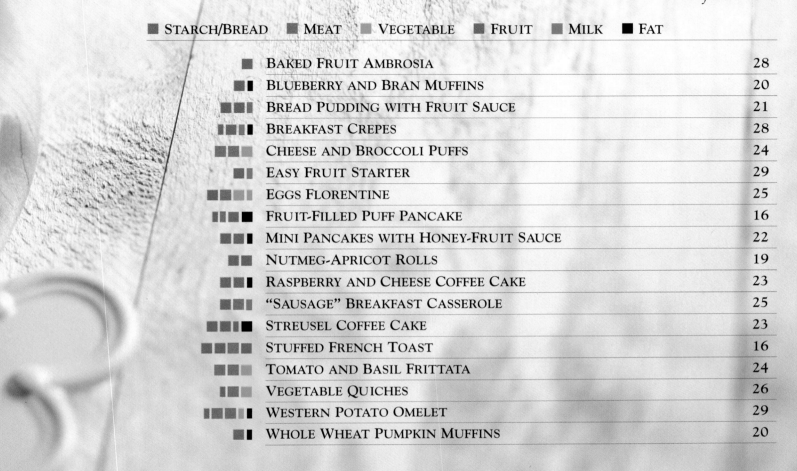

■ STARCH/BREAD ■ MEAT ■ VEGETABLE ■ FRUIT ■ MILK ■ FAT

On left: *Raspberry and Cheese Coffee Cake, page 23*

Fruit-Filled Puff Pancake

MAKES 4 SERVINGS   PREP: 10 MINUTES   BAKE: 25 MINUTES   STAND: 5 MINUTES

These puff pancakes deflate after baking to form a "bowl" just right for filling with fresh colorful fruit (pictured on page 17).

Exchanges

½ Starch
½ Very Lean Meat
1 Fruit
1 Fat

Nutrition Facts Per Serving

		Daily Values
Calories	126	6%
Total fat	5 g	7%
Saturated fat	1 g	5%
Cholesterol	1 mg	0%
Sodium	198 mg	8%
Carbohydrate	16 g	5%
Fiber	2 g	6%
Protein	5 g	

Nonstick spray coating
½ cup refrigerated or frozen egg product, thawed, or 1 whole egg plus 1 egg white
¼ cup all-purpose flour
¼ cup skim milk
1 tablespoon cooking oil
¼ teaspoon salt
2 cups fresh fruit (sliced strawberries, peeled and sliced kiwifruit, blackberries, raspberries, blueberries, seedless grapes, peeled and sliced peaches, sliced nectarines, sliced apricots, and/or pitted and halved sweet cherries)
2 tablespoons orange marmalade, warmed

1. For pancakes, spray four 4¼-inch pie plates or 4½-inch foil tart pans with nonstick coating. Set aside.

2. In a large bowl use a rotary beater or whisk to beat egg product or egg plus egg white, flour, milk, oil, and salt until smooth. Divide batter among prepared pans. Bake in a 400° oven for 25 minutes or until brown and puffy. Turn off oven; let stand in oven 5 minutes.

3. To serve, immediately after removing pancakes from oven, transfer to dinner plates. Spoon some of the fruit into center of each pancake. Drizzle fruit with warmed orange marmalade.

Stuffed French Toast

MAKES 8 SERVINGS   PREP: 20 MINUTES   BAKE: 15 MINUTES

Don't be fooled by the creamy rich-tasting filling of this French toast. It's a guilt-free mixture of fat-free cream cheese product and fruit.

Exchanges

2 Starch
1 Very Lean Meat
1 Fruit

Nutrition Facts Per Serving

		Daily Values
Calories	236	12%
Total fat	2 g	3%
Saturated fat	1 g	5%
Cholesterol	5 mg	2%
Sodium	418 mg	17%
Carbohydrate	45 g	15%
Fiber	2 g	8%
Protein	11 g	

8 1-inch-thick diagonally cut slices French bread
1 8-ounce can pineapple tidbits (juice pack)
1 8-ounce tub fat-free cream cheese
1 tablespoon apricot all-fruit spread
2 teaspoons sugar
½ teaspoon vanilla
2 egg whites
½ cup skim milk
Nonstick spray coating
⅔ cup apricot all-fruit spread
⅛ teaspoon ground nutmeg

1. Using a serrated bread knife, cut a slit through the top crust of each slice of bread to form a pocket. Set aside.

2. Drain the pineapple tidbits, reserving juice. For filling, in a bowl combine cream cheese, *half* of the pineapple, the 1 tablespoon all-fruit spread, the sugar, and vanilla. Stir until well mixed. Spoon 1 rounded tablespoon of the filling into the pocket of each slice of bread.

3. In shallow bowl stir together egg whites, milk, and *2 tablespoons* of the reserved juice. Dip the stuffed bread slices into the egg white mixture just long enough to coat both sides.

4. Spray a baking sheet with nonstick coating. Place the bread slices on the baking sheet. Bake in a 450° oven for 8 minutes. Turn the slices over. Bake 7 minutes more.

5. Meanwhile, in a small saucepan combine remaining pineapple, *2 tablespoons* of the remaining reserved juice, the ⅔ cup all-fruit spread, and the nutmeg. Cook and stir over medium heat just until fruit spread melts. Serve warm with the French toast.

Fruit-Filled Puff Pancake

NUTMEG-APRICOT ROLLS

MAKES 24   PREP: 45 MINUTES   RISE: 1½ HOURS   BAKE: 20 MINUTES

4 to 4⅓ cups all-purpose flour
2 packages active dry yeast
1 cup skim milk
⅓ cup granulated sugar
3 tablespoons margarine or butter
½ teaspoon salt
2 eggs
  Nonstick spray coating
½ cup applesauce
3 tablespoons granulated sugar
½ teaspoon ground nutmeg
⅔ cup snipped dried apricots,
    raisins, or dried cherries
1 cup sifted powdered sugar
1 teaspoon vanilla
2 to 3 teaspoons apricot nectar
    or orange juice

1. In a large mixing bowl stir together *1½ cups* of the flour and the yeast; set aside. In a medium saucepan heat and stir the milk, the ⅓ cup granulated sugar, the margarine or butter, and salt just until warm (120° to 130°) and margarine or butter almost melts. Add milk mixture and eggs to the flour mixture. Beat with an electric mixer on low to medium speed for 30 seconds, scraping the side of the bowl constantly. Beat on high speed for 3 minutes. Using a wooden spoon, stir in as much of the remaining flour as you can.

2. Turn the dough out onto a lightly floured surface. Knead in enough of the remaining flour to make a moderately soft dough that is smooth and elastic (3 to 5 minutes total). Shape the dough into a ball. Place dough in a lightly greased bowl, turning once to grease surface of the dough. Cover and let rise in a warm place until double in size (about 1 hour).

3. Punch dough down. Turn dough out onto a lightly floured surface. Divide dough in half. Cover and let rest for 10 minutes. Meanwhile, spray two 9×1½-inch round baking pans with nonstick coating.

4. Roll each half of the dough into a 12×8-inch rectangle. Spread the applesauce over the dough. In a small mixing bowl stir together the 3 tablespoons granulated sugar and the nutmeg. Sprinkle the sugar mixture over the applesauce. Sprinkle the apricots or raisins over the sugar mixture. Roll up each rectangle, jelly-roll style, starting from 1 of the long sides. Pinch seams to seal. Cut each into 12 pieces. Place pieces, cut sides down, in the prepared pans. Cover; let rise until nearly double (about 30 minutes). Or, cover with oiled waxed paper, then with plastic wrap; chill in the refrigerator for 2 to 24 hours.

5. If chilled, let stand, covered, 20 minutes at room temperature. Puncture any surface bubbles with a greased wooden toothpick. Bake in a 375° oven for 20 to 25 minutes or until golden brown. Cool in pans on wire rack for 5 minutes. Remove from pans. Cool completely on a wire rack.

6. Meanwhile, in a small mixing bowl stir together powdered sugar and vanilla. Stir in enough apricot nectar to make of drizzling consistency. Drizzle over rolls.

Flexibility is built into these rolls. Either bake them right away or refrigerate and bake them the next day (pictured on page 18).

EXCHANGES

| 1 STARCH |
| 1 FRUIT |

NUTRITION FACTS PER ROLL

		Daily Values
Calories	141	7%
Total fat	2 g	3%
Saturated fat	0 g	0%
Cholesterol	18 mg	5%
Sodium	73 mg	3%
Carbohydrate	27 g	9%
Fiber	1 g	4%
Protein	3 g	

BLUEBERRY AND BRAN MUFFINS

MAKES 12　PREP: 10 MINUTES　BAKE: 15 MINUTES

These tender, blueberry-filled muffins have about 65 fewer calories and half the fat of a standard blueberry muffin. Bran cereal bumps the fiber up to 2 grams per muffin.

EXCHANGES

| 1 STARCH |
| ½ FAT |

NUTRITION FACTS PER MUFFIN

		Daily Values
Calories	103	5%
Total fat	3 g	4%
Saturated fat	0 g	0%
Cholesterol	0 mg	0%
Sodium	176 mg	7%
Carbohydrate	20 g	6%
Fiber	2 g	9%
Protein	3 g	

Nonstick spray coating
1 cup whole bran cereal
⅔ cup skim milk
1¼ cups all-purpose flour
¼ cup packed brown sugar
2½ teaspoons baking powder
½ teaspoon ground cinnamon
¼ teaspoon salt
½ cup applesauce
¼ cup refrigerated or frozen egg product, thawed
2 tablespoons cooking oil
1 teaspoon vanilla
½ cup blueberries

1. Spray twelve 2½-inch muffin cups with nonstick coating. Set muffin cups aside.

2. In a small mixing bowl stir together bran cereal and milk. Set aside.

3. In a medium mixing bowl stir together flour, brown sugar, baking powder, cinnamon, and salt. Make a well in the center of the dry mixture.

4. In another medium mixing bowl combine the applesauce, egg product, oil, and vanilla. Stir in bran cereal mixture. Add egg product mixture all at once to the dry mixture. Stir just until moistened (batter should be lumpy). Fold in blueberries.

5. Spoon batter into the prepared muffin cups, filling each about ¾ full. Bake in a 400° oven for 15 to 20 minutes or until golden brown. Cool in muffin cups on a wire rack for 5 minutes. Remove muffins from muffin cups. Serve warm.

WHOLE WHEAT PUMPKIN MUFFINS

MAKES 12　PREP: 12 MINUTES　BAKE: 18 MINUTES

Serve these with light or fat-free cream cheese or an apricot all-fruit spread.

EXCHANGES

| 1 STARCH |
| ½ FAT |

NUTRITION FACTS PER MUFFIN

		Daily Values
Calories	106	5%
Total fat	3 g	5%
Saturated fat	1 g	5%
Cholesterol	18 mg	6%
Sodium	146 mg	6%
Carbohydrate	18 g	6%
Fiber	1 g	4%
Protein	3 g	

Nonstick spray coating
1 cup all-purpose flour
¾ cup whole wheat flour
3 tablespoons sugar
2 teaspoons baking powder
1 teaspoon pumpkin pie spice
¼ teaspoon baking soda
⅛ teaspoon salt
1 beaten egg
¾ cup skim milk
2 tablespoons margarine or butter, melted
½ cup canned pumpkin

1. Spray twelve 2½-inch muffin cups with nonstick coating. Set muffin cups aside.

2. In a large mixing bowl stir together the all-purpose flour, whole wheat flour, sugar, baking powder, pumpkin pie spice, baking soda, and salt. Make a well in the center of dry mixture. In a small mixing bowl stir together egg, milk, and margarine or butter. Stir in the pumpkin. Add egg mixture all at once to dry mixture. Using a fork, stir just until moistened (batter should be lumpy).

3. Spoon batter into prepared muffin cups, filling each ⅔ full. Bake in a 375° oven for 18 to 20 minutes or until a wooden toothpick inserted in center comes out clean. Cool in muffin cups on a wire rack for 5 minutes. Remove muffins from muffin cups. Serve warm.

BREAD PUDDING WITH FRUIT SAUCE

MAKES 6 SERVINGS   PREP: 20 MINUTES   BAKE: 35 MINUTES   STAND: 15 MINUTES

Nonstick spray coating
6 slices cinnamon-swirl bread or cinnamon-raisin bread, dried and cut into ½-inch cubes (about 4 cups)
1½ cups skim milk
¾ cup refrigerated or frozen egg product, thawed
3 tablespoons granulated sugar
1 teaspoon vanilla
¼ teaspoon ground nutmeg
1 tablespoon brown sugar
2 teaspoons cornstarch
1 5½-ounce can apricot or peach nectar

1. Spray six 6-ounce custard cups with nonstick coating. Divide the bread cubes among the custard cups.

2. In a medium mixing bowl use a rotary beater or wire whisk to beat together the milk, egg product, granulated sugar, vanilla, and nutmeg. Pour the milk mixture evenly over the bread cubes. Lightly press cubes down with fork or back of spoon.

3. Place the custard cups in a 13×9×2-inch baking pan. Place pan in oven. Carefully pour hottest tap water into the baking pan around the cups to a depth of 1 inch. Bake in a 325° oven for 35 to 40 minutes or until a knife inserted near center comes out clean. Remove the cups from the baking pan. Let stand for 15 to 20 minutes.

4. Meanwhile, for sauce, in a small saucepan combine brown sugar and cornstarch. Stir in nectar. Cook and stir over medium heat until thickened and bubbly. Reduce heat. Cook and stir for 2 minutes more. Loosen edges of puddings. Invert into dessert bowls or plates. Serve bread puddings warm with sauce.

Quickly dry the bread slices by placing them in a single layer on a baking sheet in a 325° oven for about 10 minutes, turning once. Cool on a wire rack; cut into cubes.

EXCHANGES

2 STARCH
½ VERY LEAN MEAT

NUTRITION FACTS PER SERVING

		Daily Values
Calories	171	8%
Total fat	2 g	3%
Saturated fat	1 g	5%
Cholesterol	1 mg	0%
Sodium	190 mg	7%
Carbohydrate	30 g	9%
Fiber	0 g	0%
Protein	8 g	

Using Egg Substitutes

You can enjoy tasty low-cholesterol versions of your favorite omelets, custards, and other egg-based foods by incorporating egg substitutes into your cooking. These eggs in disguise are based mostly on egg whites and contain less fat than whole eggs and no cholesterol. Besides obvious egg dishes like omelets, try egg substitutes in yeast breads, muffins, cakes, cookies, casseroles, sauces, puddings, and custards. Avoid using egg substitutes in cream puffs and popovers because they won't puff or pop. Check the package directions before using any egg substitute.

Make your own homemade egg substitute by using 2 egg whites for each whole egg called for in a recipe. If the recipe requires a lot of eggs or it needs a little richness or color, use 2 egg whites and 1 whole egg for every 2 whole eggs.

MINI PANCAKES WITH HONEY-FRUIT SAUCE

MAKES 7 SERVINGS (28 PANCAKES)   PREP: 20 MINUTES   COOK: 20 MINUTES

The honey and fruit sauce is what makes these mini flapjacks a special breakfast treat.

EXCHANGES

| 1 STARCH |
| 1 FRUIT |
| ½ FAT |

NUTRITION FACTS PER SERVING

		Daily Values
Calories	171	8%
Total fat	3 g	4%
Saturated fat	1 g	5%
Cholesterol	2 mg	0%
Sodium	290 mg	12%
Carbohydrate	31 g	10%
Fiber	1 g	3%
Protein	5 g	

1¼ cups all-purpose flour
1 tablespoon sugar
1 teaspoon baking powder
½ teaspoon baking soda
¼ teaspoon salt
1½ cups buttermilk
¼ cup refrigerated or frozen egg product, thawed
1 tablespoon cooking oil
Nonstick spray coating
1 recipe Honey-Fruit Sauce

1. For pancakes, in a medium mixing bowl stir together the flour, sugar, baking powder, baking soda, and salt. In another mixing bowl combine the buttermilk, egg product, and oil. Add to the flour mixture all at once. Stir the mixture just until combined but still slightly lumpy.

2. Spray an unheated nonstick griddle or nonstick heavy skillet with nonstick coating. For each pancake, pour about 1 tablespoon batter onto hot griddle or skillet. Cook until pancakes are golden brown on both sides, turning when pancakes have bubbly surfaces and slightly dry edges (about 1 minute per side). Serve pancakes with warm Honey-Fruit Sauce.

Honey-Fruit Sauce: In a small saucepan stir together ¾ cup *unsweetened pineapple juice* or *orange juice*, 2 tablespoons *honey*, 2 teaspoons *cornstarch*, and ⅛ teaspoon *ground ginger*. Cook and stir over medium heat until thickened and bubbly. Cook and stir for 2 minutes more. Stir in 1 cup sliced *strawberries*, *raspberries*, and/or *blueberries*.

Note: Wrap, label, and freeze any leftover pancakes. To reheat, place 4 frozen mini pancakes in a single layer on a microwave-safe plate. Cook, uncovered, on 100% power (high) for 45 seconds to 1¼ minutes or until heated through, turning pancakes over after 30 seconds.

A.M. Fiber

One of the easiest ways to add more fiber to your diet is with a healthy dose of cereal, whole grain bread, or fresh juicy fruits at breakfast. Take a good look at the foods below to help you make smart fiber-rich choices.

Cereal
Whole bran (⅓ cup) 9 g
100% bran (½ cup) 8 g
40% bran flakes (⅔ cup) 4 g

Granola, homemade (¼ cup) 3 g
Raisin bran (½ cup) 3 g
Oatmeal (¾ cup cooked) 3 g
Shredded wheat (1 biscuit) 2 g
Wheat flakes (¾ cup) 2 g

Breads
Whole wheat bread (1 slice) 2 g
Bran muffin, homemade (1 whole) 3 g
Plain English muffin (1 whole) 2 g
Plain bagel (1 whole) 1 g
White bread (1 slice) 1 g

Fruit
Dried prunes (6) 3 g
Raisins (½ cup) 2 g
Orange (1) 3 g
Apple (1 with skin) 3 g
Strawberries (½ cup) 2 g
Banana (1) 2 g
Cantaloupe, cubed (1 cup) 1 g
Grapefruit (½) 1 g

RASPBERRY AND CHEESE COFFEE CAKE
MAKES 10 SERVINGS   PREP: 20 MINUTES   BAKE: 30 MINUTES

Nonstick spray coating
1¼ cups all-purpose flour
1¼ teaspoons baking powder
1 teaspoon finely shredded lemon
   or orange peel
¼ teaspoon baking soda
¼ teaspoon salt
¾ cup granulated sugar
3 tablespoons margarine or
   butter, softened
¼ cup refrigerated or frozen egg
   product, thawed
1 teaspoon vanilla
½ cup buttermilk
2 ounces reduced-fat cream
   cheese (Neufchâtel)
¼ cup granulated sugar
2 tablespoons refrigerated or
   frozen egg product, thawed
1 cup raspberries or thinly sliced
   apricots or nectarines*
   Raspberries or thinly sliced
   apricots or nectarines
   (optional)
   Sifted powdered sugar

1. Spray a 9×1½-inch round baking pan with nonstick coating. Set aside. In a medium mixing bowl stir together the flour, baking powder, lemon or orange peel, baking soda, and salt. Set aside.

2. In a medium mixing bowl beat the ¾ cup granulated sugar and margarine or butter with an electric mixer on medium to high speed until combined. Add the ¼ cup egg product and the vanilla. Beat on low to medium speed for 1 minute. Alternately add the flour mixture and buttermilk to the egg mixture, beating just until combined after each addition. Pour into prepared pan.

3. In a small mixing bowl beat the cream cheese and the ¼ cup granulated sugar on medium to high speed until combined. Add the 2 tablespoons egg product. Beat until combined. Arrange the 1 cup raspberries over the batter in the pan. Pour the cream cheese mixture over all. Bake in a 375° oven for 30 to 35 minutes or until a wooden toothpick inserted near center comes out clean. Cool slightly on wire rack. Serve warm. If desired, top with additional raspberries. Dust with powdered sugar.

*Note: If you like, substitute well-drained, thinly sliced canned apricots or peach slices for the fresh fruit.

With fruit and a cheesecake-like topping, you'll never miss the fat in this calorie-reduced coffee cake (pictured on page 14).

EXCHANGES
| 2 STARCH |
| ½ FAT |

NUTRITION FACTS PER SERVING
		Daily Values
Calories	195	9%
Total fat	5 g	8%
Saturated fat	2 g	10%
Cholesterol	5 mg	1%
Sodium	223 mg	9%
Carbohydrate	33 g	11%
Fiber	1 g	2%
Protein	4 g	

STREUSEL COFFEE CAKE
MAKES 9 SERVINGS   PREP: 20 MINUTES   BAKE: 20 MINUTES

Nonstick spray coating
3 tablespoons brown sugar
1 tablespoon all-purpose flour
1 teaspoon ground cinnamon
1 tablespoon margarine or
   reduced-fat cream cheese
   (Neufchâtel)
¼ cup finely chopped walnuts
1½ cups all-purpose flour
¾ cup granulated sugar
2 teaspoons baking powder
⅛ teaspoon salt
½ cup skim milk
1 slightly beaten egg white
3 tablespoons cooking oil

1. Spray a 9×9×2-inch baking pan with nonstick coating. Set pan aside.

2. For streusel topping, in a small mixing bowl stir together the brown sugar, the 1 tablespoon flour, and the cinnamon. Cut in the margarine or cream cheese until crumbly. Stir in walnuts. Set topping aside.

3. For cake, in a medium mixing bowl stir together the 1½ cups flour, the granulated sugar, baking powder, and salt. In another mixing bowl stir together the milk, egg white, and cooking oil. Add to flour mixture, stirring just until combined. Pour batter into the prepared pan. Sprinkle the streusel topping over batter.

4. Bake in a 350° oven about 20 minutes or until a wooden toothpick inserted near the center comes out clean. Cool slightly on wire rack. Serve warm.

If you have leftovers you'd like to warm up, wrap the cake in foil and reheat it in a 350° oven for 15 minutes.

EXCHANGES
| 2 STARCH |
| ½ FRUIT |
| 1 FAT |

NUTRITION FACTS PER SERVING
		Daily Values
Calories	231	12%
Total fat	8 g	12%
Saturated fat	1 g	5%
Cholesterol	0 mg	0%
Sodium	124 mg	5%
Carbohydrate	37 g	12%
Fiber	1 g	4%
Protein	3 g	

CHEESE AND BROCCOLI PUFFS

MAKES 4 SERVINGS   PREP: 20 MINUTES   BAKE: 20 MINUTES

These broccoli-filled soufflés start with reduced-fat soup, adding flavor and ease.

EXCHANGES
2 MEDIUM-FAT MEAT
1 VEGETABLE

NUTRITION FACTS PER SERVING		
		Daily Values
Calories	164	8%
Total fat	9 g	14%
Saturated fat	4 g	19%
Cholesterol	229 mg	76%
Sodium	299 mg	12%
Carbohydrate	5 g	1%
Fiber	1 g	5%
Protein	14 g	

1 cup chopped broccoli flowerets
2 green onions, sliced
4 beaten egg yolks
½ of a 10¾-ounce can (⅔ cup) reduced-fat and reduced-sodium condensed cream of mushroom or broccoli soup
¾ cup shredded reduced-fat cheddar or Swiss cheese (3 ounces)
½ teaspoon dried dillweed
4 egg whites
⅛ teaspoon cream of tartar

1. In a medium covered saucepan cook broccoli and green onions in a small amount of boiling water for 2 to 3 minutes or until crisp-tender. Drain. Set aside.

2. In a medium mixing bowl combine egg yolks, soup, cheese, and dillweed. Stir in broccoli-onion mixture.

3. In a large mixing bowl beat egg whites and cream of tartar until stiff peaks form (tips stand straight). Gently fold together egg whites and broccoli mixture. Spoon into 4 ungreased 10- to 12-ounce soufflé dishes.*

4. Bake in a 350° oven for 20 to 25 minutes or until a knife inserted near the center of each comes out clean. Serve immediately.

*Note: To make one large soufflé, turn mixture into an ungreased 1½-quart soufflé dish. Bake in a 350° oven about 40 minutes or until a knife inserted near the center comes out clean. Serve immediately.

TOMATO AND BASIL FRITTATA

MAKES 2 SERVINGS   PREP: 15 MINUTES   BAKE: 7 MINUTES

If you don't have an oven-going skillet for this recipe, simply use foil to cover the handle of an 8-inch skillet.

EXCHANGES
2 LEAN MEAT
1 VEGETABLE

NUTRITION FACTS PER SERVING		
		Daily Values
Calories	149	7%
Total fat	6 g	9%
Saturated fat	2 g	10%
Cholesterol	117 mg	39%
Sodium	428 mg	18%
Carbohydrate	5 g	2%
Fiber	1 g	4%
Protein	17 g	

5 egg whites
1 egg
1 tablespoon snipped fresh basil or ½ teaspoon dried basil, crushed
⅛ teaspoon salt
   Dash pepper
   Nonstick spray coating
½ cup chopped fresh spinach
2 green onions, sliced
1 clove garlic, minced
1 small tomato, chopped
¼ cup shredded reduced-fat cheddar cheese (1 ounce)

1. In a medium bowl lightly beat together egg whites and whole egg. Stir in basil, salt, and pepper; set aside.

2. Spray an unheated 8-inch oven-going skillet with nonstick coating. Preheat the skillet over medium heat. Add spinach, green onions, and garlic. Cook for 1 to 2 minutes or until spinach begins to wilt. Remove skillet from heat; drain, if necessary.

3. Pour egg mixture over spinach mixture in the skillet. Bake, uncovered, in a 350° oven for 6 to 8 minutes or until eggs are set. Sprinkle with chopped tomato and cheese. Bake for 1 to 2 minutes more or until the cheese melts. Cut the frittata into wedges to serve.

"SAUSAGE" BREAKFAST CASSEROLE

MAKES 6 SERVINGS   PREP: 20 MINUTES   CHILL: 4 HOURS   BAKE: 35 MINUTES   STAND: 5 MINUTES

Nonstick spray coating
1½ cups sliced fresh mushrooms
4 ounces ground raw turkey
¼ teaspoon dried sage, crushed
⅛ teaspoon ground red pepper
⅛ teaspoon ground cumin
1 clove garlic, minced
Nonstick spray coating
8 ½-inch-thick slices French bread or other firm-textured bread
1 cup fat-free cottage cheese
1 cup evaporated skim milk
3 egg whites
1 egg
¾ teaspoon dry mustard
2 green onions, sliced
2 tablespoons finely shredded or grated Parmesan cheese

1. Spray an unheated medium skillet with nonstick coating. Cook mushrooms, turkey, sage, red pepper, cumin, and garlic in skillet until turkey is no longer pink. Drain well.

2. Spray a 2-quart rectangular baking dish with nonstick coating. Place bread slices in the prepared baking dish, cutting as necessary to fit. Sprinkle the turkey mixture over the bread slices.

3. In a blender container or food processor bowl, combine the cottage cheese, evaporated skim milk, egg whites, egg, and dry mustard. Cover and blend or process until smooth. Pour over turkey mixture in baking dish. Lightly press bread down with a fork or the back of a spoon. Cover and refrigerate for 4 to 24 hours. Bake, uncovered, in a 350° oven about 35 minutes or until a knife inserted near the center comes out clean. Sprinkle with green onions and Parmesan cheese. Let stand for 5 minutes before serving.

Ground turkey with traditional sausage seasonings produces a great sausage flavor without the fat and sodium.

EXCHANGES

| 1 STARCH |
| 1 LEAN MEAT |
| ½ MILK |

NUTRITION FACTS PER SERVING

		Daily Values
Calories	190	9%
Total fat	4 g	6%
Saturated fat	1 g	5%
Cholesterol	47 mg	15%
Sodium	432 mg	17%
Carbohydrate	21 g	7%
Fiber	0 g	1%
Protein	16 g	

EGGS FLORENTINE

MAKES 4 SERVINGS   PREP: 25 MINUTES

Nonstick spray coating
1 cup sliced fresh mushrooms
3 green onions, sliced
¼ cup shredded carrot
1 cup skim milk
4 teaspoons cornstarch
¾ teaspoon instant chicken bouillon granules
⅛ teaspoon dried tarragon or marjoram, crushed
½ of a 10-ounce package frozen chopped spinach, thawed and well drained
2 English muffins, split and toasted
4 eggs
Pepper

1. For sauce, spray an unheated medium saucepan with nonstick coating. Preheat saucepan over medium heat. Add mushrooms, green onions, and shredded carrot. Cook and stir until tender. Stir the milk into cornstarch. Stir into vegetable mixture in saucepan; add bouillon granules and tarragon. Cook and stir until thickened and bubbly. Cook and stir for 2 minutes more.

2. Remove about ¾ cup of the sauce; cover and keep warm. Add spinach to the remaining sauce in saucepan. Heat through. Spoon the spinach mixture onto the English muffin halves. Keep warm in a 300° oven.

3. Meanwhile, in another medium saucepan add *water* to half-fill the pan. Bring to boiling. Break *one* egg into a measuring cup. Carefully slide egg into simmering water. Repeat with remaining eggs. Simmer, uncovered, for 4 to 5 minutes or until egg yolks are just set. Remove eggs with a slotted spoon.

4. Place 1 egg on each muffin half; sprinkle lightly with pepper. Top each egg with some of the reserved sauce.

For a weekend morning treat, serve these poached eggs on English muffins with the herbed vegetable sauce.

EXCHANGES

| 1 STARCH |
| 1 MEDIUM-FAT MEAT |
| 1½ VEGETABLE |

NUTRITION FACTS PER SERVING

		Daily Values
Calories	207	10%
Total fat	6 g	9%
Saturated fat	2 g	10%
Cholesterol	214 mg	71%
Sodium	488 mg	20%
Carbohydrate	25 g	8%
Fiber	2 g	6%
Protein	13 g	

VEGETABLE QUICHES

MAKES 6 SERVINGS   PREP: 25 MINUTES   BAKE: 25 MINUTES   STAND: 5 MINUTES

Using tortillas for the crust and fat-free egg product, reduced-fat cheese, and evaporated skim milk for the filling cuts the fat down to just 4 grams per serving in these mini quiches (pictured on page 27). A traditional quiche has more than 20 grams of fat per serving.

EXCHANGES

| ½ STARCH |
| 1 LEAN MEAT |
| 1 VEGETABLE |

NUTRITION FACTS PER SERVING

		Daily Values
Calories	133	6%
Total fat	4 g	5%
Saturated fat	1 g	5%
Cholesterol	6 mg	1%
Sodium	333 mg	13%
Carbohydrate	14 g	4%
Fiber	1 g	3%
Protein	10 g	

Nonstick spray coating
3 7- or 8-inch flour tortillas
2 ounces shredded reduced-fat Swiss, cheddar, or mozzarella cheese (½ cup)
1 cup broccoli flowerets
½ of a small red sweet pepper, cut into thin strips (½ cup)
2 green onions, sliced
1 8-ounce carton refrigerated or frozen egg product, thawed (about 1 cup)
¾ cup evaporated skim milk
¼ teaspoon dried thyme, crushed
⅛ teaspoon salt
⅛ teaspoon black pepper
Thin strips red sweet pepper (optional)

1. Spray three 6- to 7-inch individual round baking dishes or pans* with nonstick coating. Carefully press tortillas into dishes or pans. Sprinkle with cheese.

2. In a small covered saucepan cook the broccoli, the ½ cup sweet pepper strips, and the green onions in a small amount of *boiling water* about 3 minutes or until crisp-tender. Drain well. Sprinkle cooked vegetables over cheese in baking dishes.

3. In a medium mixing bowl stir together egg product, evaporated skim milk, thyme, salt, and black pepper. Pour over vegetables in baking dishes. Place on a baking sheet. Bake in a 375° oven for 25 to 30 minutes or until puffed and a knife inserted near center of each comes out clean. Let stand 5 minutes before serving. If desired, garnish with additional strips of sweet pepper.

*Note: Or, spray six 6-ounce custard cups with nonstick coating. Cut each tortilla into 6 wedges. To form crust, press 3 tortilla wedges into each custard cup with points toward center. Tortillas do not have to cover cups completely. Continue as above.

BREAKFAST CREPES

MAKES 4 SERVINGS   PREP: 30 MINUTES

You can stack the crepes between waxed paper and place them in an airtight container. Freeze them for up to 4 months.

EXCHANGES

½ STARCH
1 FRUIT
½ MILK
½ FAT

NUTRITION FACTS PER SERVING

		Daily Values
Calories	157	7%
Total fat	2 g	3%
Saturated fat	0 g	0%
Cholesterol	1 mg	0%
Sodium	130 mg	5%
Carbohydrate	31 g	10%
Fiber	3 g	10%
Protein	6 g	

⅔ cup skim milk
⅓ cup all-purpose flour
3 tablespoons refrigerated or frozen egg product, thawed
1 teaspoon cooking oil
⅛ teaspoon salt
  Nonstick spray coating
  Cooking oil (optional)
¼ cup orange marmalade
½ cup vanilla, orange, or lemon fat-free yogurt
1½ cups sliced strawberries

1. In a mixing bowl stir together milk, flour, egg product, the 1 teaspoon oil, and salt. Beat with a rotary beater until well mixed.

2. Spray an unheated 6-inch nonstick skillet with nonstick coating. Heat skillet over medium heat. Remove skillet from heat. Spoon 2 tablespoons of the batter into the skillet. Lift and tilt skillet to spread batter. Return to heat. Brown on 1 side only (30 to 60 seconds). (Or, cook on an inverted crepe maker according to manufacturer's directions.) Invert pan over paper towels; remove crepe. Repeat with remaining batter, making 8 crepes total. If necessary, lightly brush the skillet with cooking oil to prevent crepes from sticking.*

3. In a small saucepan cook and stir the marmalade over medium-low heat until melted. In a small mixing bowl stir together yogurt and *1 tablespoon* of the orange marmalade. Gently fold strawberries into the yogurt mixture. Spoon some of the strawberry mixture down the center of each crepe. Roll up. Drizzle with remaining orange marmalade.

*__Note:__ Spraying a hot skillet with nonstick coating is not recommended.

BAKED FRUIT AMBROSIA

MAKES 4 SERVINGS   PREP: 15 MINUTES   BAKE: 10 MINUTES

For a simpler version of this eye-opening side dish, skip the orange cups. Instead, spoon the fruit mixture into four 6-ounce custard cups.

EXCHANGES

1 FRUIT

NUTRITION FACTS PER SERVING

		Daily Values
Calories	74	3%
Total fat	0 g	0%
Saturated fat	0 g	0%
Cholesterol	0 mg	0%
Sodium	2 mg	0%
Carbohydrate	18 g	6%
Fiber	1 g	4%
Protein	1 g	

2 large oranges
1 8-ounce can pineapple tidbits, drained
1 tablespoon honey
¼ teaspoon ground cinnamon
1 tablespoon coconut

1. For orange cups, cut oranges in half from blossom to stem end. Using a grapefruit knife or spoon, remove orange sections and membrane, leaving orange peel intact. Discard membrane; reserve orange sections. Cut sections into bite-size pieces.

2. In a small bowl place orange sections cut into bite-size pieces. Add pineapple, honey, and cinnamon and stir together. Place orange cups in a 2-quart square baking dish. Spoon fruit mixture into orange cups. Sprinkle with coconut. Bake in a 350° oven for 10 to 15 minutes or until fruit is heated through and coconut is golden brown. Serve warm.

WESTERN POTATO OMELET

MAKES 2 SERVINGS   PREP: 10 MINUTES   COOK: 10 MINUTES

Nonstick spray coating
¼ **cup diced potato or frozen diced hash brown potatoes, thawed**
¼ **cup chopped red or green sweet pepper**
2 **tablespoons chopped onion**
1 **slice Canadian-style bacon (1 ounce), diced, or 3 tablespoons diced lean cooked ham**
1 **to 2 tablespoons water**
¾ **cup refrigerated or frozen egg product, thawed**
¼ **teaspoon dried oregano, thyme, or marjoram, crushed**
⅛ **teaspoon black pepper**
1 **teaspoon margarine or butter**
2 **tablespoons shredded reduced-fat cheddar cheese**

1. Spray an unheated medium nonstick skillet with nonstick coating. Heat skillet over medium heat. Add potatoes, sweet pepper, onion, and Canadian-style bacon or ham to skillet. Sprinkle with 1 tablespoon water. Cover and cook over medium heat for 4 to 5 minutes or until vegetables are tender, stirring once or twice. (If necessary, add the additional tablespoon of water to prevent sticking.) Remove potato mixture from skillet. Set aside; keep warm.

2. In a small mixing bowl use a fork to beat together egg product, oregano, and black pepper. In a medium skillet melt margarine or butter. Pour egg product mixture into hot skillet. Cook over medium heat. As mixture sets, use a spatula to push cooked mixture toward center, tilting pan so uncooked mixture flows underneath to the pan surface. When mixture is set but still shiny, sprinkle the potato mixture on half of the omelet. Sprinkle cheese over potato mixture. Fold unfilled half of the omelet over filling. Slide onto a serving plate. Cut in half to serve.

Thought omelets were off your healthy menu? Not so, with this potato- and vegetable-filled version made with fat-free egg substitute and reduced-fat cheese.

EXCHANGES

½ STARCH
2 LEAN MEAT
½ VEGETABLE
½ FAT

NUTRITION FACTS PER SERVING

		Daily Values
Calories	180	8%
Total fat	8 g	12%
Saturated fat	2 g	10%
Cholesterol	14 mg	4%
Sodium	460 mg	19%
Carbohydrate	9 g	2%
Fiber	1 g	3%
Protein	18 g	

EASY FRUIT STARTER

MAKES 2 SERVINGS   PREP: 15 MINUTES

1 **cup halved strawberries, chopped peeled peaches, or chopped nectarines**
1 **6- or 8-ounce carton strawberry or peach fat-free yogurt**
⅓ **cup skim milk**
1 **tablespoon honey or brown sugar**
2 **large ice cubes or ¼ cup crushed ice**

1. In a blender container combine fruit, yogurt, milk, and honey or brown sugar. Cover and blend until smooth.

2. With the blender running, add ice cubes, 1 at a time, through the opening in lid. (Or, add crushed ice through opening in lid.) Blend until smooth. Pour into glasses. Serve immediately.

This easy blender drink makes a great snack or a quick breakfast on busy mornings. Change the fresh fruit and yogurt flavors to fit your personal favorites.

EXCHANGES

1 FRUIT
½ MILK

NUTRITION FACTS PER SERVING

		Daily Values
Calories	109	5%
Total fat	0 g	0%
Saturated fat	0 g	0%
Cholesterol	3 mg	1%
Sodium	88 mg	3%
Carbohydrate	23 g	7%
Fiber	1 g	5%
Protein	5 g	

MAIN DISHES

■ STARCH/BREAD ■ MEAT ■ VEGETABLE ■ FRUIT ■ MILK ■ FAT

Dish	Page
BEAN AND CORN TAMALE PIE	65
CHICKEN IN PUMPKIN PEPPER MOLE	33
CHICKEN TERIYAKI WITH SUMMER FRUIT	32
CHICKEN WITH MUSHROOM SAUCE	36
CHILI-SAUCED PASTA	65
CHUTNEY-SAUCED CHICKEN	33
CITRUS CHICKEN SANDWICHES	38
CITRUS-TARRAGON SALMON STEAKS	57
CITRUS-TEQUILA FAJITAS	47
CREAMY FISH CHOWDER	59
CRISPY BAKED HALIBUT	60
CURRIED LAMB	55
CURRIED LENTILS AND VEGETABLES	66
FRESH TOMATO AND TURKEY PIZZA	41
GARDEN TURKEY BURGERS	40
GRILLED VEAL CHOPS	54
HAM AND BEAN SOUP	51
HAM AND BROCCOLI SOUFFLÉ	50
HEARTY BEEF STEW	44
HONEY-GLAZED SALMON	58
HONEY HAM SALAD	51
HOT ORIENTAL BEEF AND PASTA	43
HOT TURKEY SUB SANDWICHES	39
JAMAICAN CHICKEN SALAD	38
LAMB KABOBS	55
LEMON PEPPER STEAK	45
ORANGE BARBECUED TURKEY	40
ORANGE CHICKEN AND BROCCOLI	32
ORANGE-GLAZED PORK CHOPS	48
PINTO BEAN AND CHEESE BURRITOS	67
PORK AND FRUIT SALAD	53
PORK WITH APPLE-SOUR CREAM SAUCE	48
QUICK CREOLE	59
SALMON HASH WITH POTATOES AND PEPPERS	63
SALMON WITH FRUIT SALSA	57
SPINACH- AND RICOTTA-STUFFED TOMATOES	67
SPINACH CHICKEN WITH DIJON SAUCE	36
SPINACH SOUFFLÉ IN CORNMEAL CREPES	68
STEAK WITH MARSALA SAUCE	45
TOMATO-STUFFED CHICKEN ROLLS	35
TUNA-PASTA SALAD	63
TURKEY TENDERLOINS IN PAPRIKA SAUCE	41
VEAL PARMIGIANA	54
VEGETABLE LASAGNA	64
VEGETABLE-MACARONI CASSEROLE	66
ZUPPA DI PESCE	60

On left: *Chicken Teriyaki with Summer Fruit, page 32*

Chicken Teriyaki with Summer Fruit

MAKES 4 SERVINGS   PREP: 20 MINUTES   GRILL: 12 MINUTES

Nectarines and peaches often are hard when you purchase them. To ripen them to juicy perfection, place them in a paper bag at room temperature for a day or two. (Chicken teriyaki pictured on page 30.)

Exchanges
3 Very Lean Meat
1½ Fruit

Nutrition Facts Per Serving

		Daily Values
Calories	200	10%
Total fat	4 g	5%
Saturated fat	1 g	4%
Cholesterol	59 mg	19%
Sodium	136 mg	5%
Carbohydrate	20 g	6%
Fiber	2 g	6%
Protein	22 g	

2 cups finely chopped nectarines, finely chopped plums, and/or blueberries
2 tablespoons orange marmalade, melted
1 tablespoon lemon or lime juice
½ teaspoon grated gingerroot
¼ teaspoon toasted sesame oil
  Few dashes bottled hot pepper sauce
4 medium skinless, boneless chicken breast halves (about 1 pound total)
1 tablespoon orange marmalade
1 tablespoon reduced-sodium teriyaki sauce
  Fresh strawberries (optional)
  Flowering kale (optional)

1. In a small mixing bowl stir together the fruit, the 2 tablespoons melted orange marmalade, the lemon or lime juice, gingerroot, sesame oil, and hot pepper sauce. Set aside.

2. Rinse chicken; pat dry with paper towels. In a small bowl stir together the 1 tablespoon orange marmalade and the teriyaki sauce; brush over chicken breasts. Grill on the rack of an uncovered grill directly over medium-hot coals for 12 to 15 minutes or until tender and no longer pink, turning once. (Or, place on the unheated rack of a broiler pan. Broil 4 to 5 inches from the heat for 12 to 15 minutes or until tender and no longer pink, turning once.) Serve with the fruit mixture. If desired, garnish with fresh strawberries and kale.

Orange Chicken and Broccoli

MAKES 4 SERVINGS   PREP: 35 MINUTES   MARINATE: 20 MINUTES

Look for tamari sauce in Oriental markets and large grocery stores. If you can't find it, soy sauce will make a good substitute.

Exchanges
1½ Starch
2 Very Lean Meat
2 Vegetable
½ Fat

Nutrition Facts Per Serving

		Daily Values
Calories	293	15%
Total fat	7 g	11%
Saturated fat	1 g	5%
Cholesterol	45 mg	15%
Sodium	312 mg	13%
Carbohydrate	37 g	12%
Fiber	4 g	16%
Protein	21 g	

1 tablespoon tamari or soy sauce
1 tablespoon dry sherry
1 teaspoon grated gingerroot
12 ounces skinless, boneless chicken breasts, cut into 1-inch pieces
1 cup orange juice
1 tablespoon cornstarch
  Nonstick spray coating
3 cups sliced broccoli
1 medium onion, sliced
1 tablespoon cooking oil
2 cups hot cooked brown rice
  Orange slices, halved (optional)

1. For marinade, in a medium mixing bowl combine tamari or soy sauce, sherry, and gingerroot. Add chicken pieces, stirring to coat. Cover and refrigerate about 20 minutes. Drain, reserving marinade. For sauce, in a small mixing bowl combine reserved marinade, orange juice, and cornstarch; set aside.

2. Spray an unheated wok or large skillet with nonstick coating. Preheat over medium-high heat. Add the broccoli and onion. Stir-fry about 3 minutes or until broccoli is crisp-tender. Remove from wok. Add oil to wok; add drained chicken. Stir-fry for 2 to 3 minutes or until chicken is tender and no longer pink. Push chicken to side of wok.

3. Stir sauce and add to wok. Cook, stirring constantly, until thickened and bubbly. Stir broccoli mixture and chicken into sauce. Cook and stir 1 to 2 minutes more or until heated through. Serve with rice. If desired, garnish with orange slices.

CHUTNEY-SAUCED CHICKEN

MAKES 6 SERVINGS   PREP: 15 MINUTES   BAKE: 20 MINUTES

Nonstick spray coating
6 small skinless, boneless chicken breast halves (about 1¼ pounds total)
½ cup cornflake crumbs
1 tablespoon grated Parmesan cheese
1 teaspoon paprika
¼ teaspoon pepper
1 egg white
¼ cup skim milk
½ cup chopped fresh mango, peach, or pineapple
¼ cup mango chutney
3 to 4 tablespoons orange juice or pineapple juice

1. Spray a baking sheet with nonstick coating. Set aside. Rinse chicken; pat dry with paper towels. In a shallow dish stir together cornflake crumbs, Parmesan cheese, paprika, and pepper. In another shallow dish lightly beat together egg white and milk.

2. Dip each chicken breast half in milk mixture. Roll in crumb mixture until well coated. Place on prepared baking sheet. Bake in a 375° oven for 20 to 25 minutes or until chicken is tender and no longer pink.

3. Meanwhile, stir together the chopped fresh fruit and the chutney. Stir in enough juice to make of desired consistency. To serve, spoon fruit mixture over chicken.

Chopped fresh fruit makes the chutney topping for this crispy oven-fried chicken extra chunky.

EXCHANGES

2½ VERY LEAN MEAT
1 FRUIT

NUTRITION FACTS PER SERVING

		Daily Values
Calories	164	8%
Total fat	3 g	4%
Saturated fat	1 g	4%
Cholesterol	51 mg	16%
Sodium	128 mg	5%
Carbohydrate	13 g	4%
Fiber	1 g	2%
Protein	20 g	

CHICKEN IN PUMPKIN PEPPER MOLE

MAKES 6 SERVINGS   PREP: 45 MINUTES

2 dried ancho or pasilla peppers or ¼ teaspoon crushed red pepper flakes
¼ cup water
6 medium skinless, boneless chicken breast halves (about 1½ pounds total)
Salt
Black pepper
¼ cup chicken broth
1 medium tomato, cut up
1 medium onion, cut up
⅓ cup pumpkin seeds or blanched almonds, toasted
2 cloves garlic
1 tablespoon sugar
½ teaspoon salt
½ teaspoon ground coriander
¼ teaspoon ground cinnamon
Warmed flour tortillas (optional)

1. Cut up ancho or pasilla peppers; discard stems and seeds. In a small saucepan combine peppers and water. Bring to boiling; remove from heat. Let peppers stand for 30 minutes; drain. Set aside.

2. Rinse the chicken; pat dry with paper towels. Arrange chicken in a large skillet; add a small amount of *water*. Sprinkle chicken with salt and pepper. Bring water to boiling; reduce heat. Simmer, covered, about 12 minutes or until the chicken is tender and no longer pink.

3. Meanwhile, for sauce, in a blender container or food processor bowl, combine the peppers or red pepper flakes, broth, tomato, onion, pumpkin seeds or almonds, garlic, sugar, the ½ teaspoon salt, the coriander, and cinnamon. Cover and blend or process until nearly smooth, scraping down sides of container as needed. Transfer to a small saucepan and bring to boiling over medium heat. Remove from heat.

4. To serve, spoon the sauce over the chicken. If desired, serve with warmed flour tortillas.

Choose the chili peppers according to your heat preferences—ancho peppers range from mild to medium-hot and pasilla peppers are very hot.

EXCHANGES

3 VERY LEAN MEAT
1 VEGETABLE
1 FAT

NUTRITION FACTS PER SERVING

		Daily Values
Calories	184	9%
Total fat	7 g	11%
Saturated fat	2 g	10%
Cholesterol	59 mg	20%
Sodium	293 mg	12%
Carbohydrate	6 g	2%
Fiber	1 g	4%
Protein	24 g	

TOMATO-STUFFED CHICKEN ROLLS

MAKES 4 SERVINGS   PREP: 20 MINUTES   BAKE: 20 MINUTES

4 small skinless, boneless chicken breast halves (about 12 ounces total)
1 medium tomato, seeded and chopped (about ½ cup)
2 tablespoons grated Parmesan cheese
¼ teaspoon dried Italian seasoning, oregano, or basil, crushed
⅛ teaspoon pepper
1 beaten egg white
1 tablespoon water
⅓ cup cornflake crumbs
½ teaspoon dried Italian seasoning, oregano, or basil, crushed
 Nonstick spray coating
 Purchased reduced-sodium spaghetti sauce, warmed (optional)
 Hot cooked fettuccine or other pasta (optional)

1. Rinse chicken; pat dry with paper towels. Place each breast half between 2 pieces of plastic wrap. Working from the center to the edges, pound lightly with the flat side of a meat mallet into a rectangle about ⅛ inch thick. Remove plastic wrap.

2. Sprinkle chicken rectangles with the tomato, Parmesan cheese, the ¼ teaspoon herb, and pepper. Fold in long sides of each chicken rectangle and roll up, jelly-roll style, to enclose filling. Secure with wooden toothpicks.

3. In a shallow dish combine the egg white and water. In another shallow dish combine cornflake crumbs and the ½ teaspoon herb. Dip each roll into the egg mixture. Roll in the crumb mixture to coat.

4. Spray a 2-quart square baking dish with nonstick coating. Place chicken rolls in dish. Bake in a 400° oven for 20 to 25 minutes or until chicken is tender and no longer pink. Remove toothpicks. If desired, slice chicken rolls and serve with warmed spaghetti sauce over hot cooked pasta.

Serve these tomato- and cheese-stuffed rolls with pasta and steamed asparagus spears for a healthful yet tasty meal (pictured on page 34).

EXCHANGES

| 2½ VERY LEAN MEAT |
| ½ VEGETABLE |

NUTRITION FACTS PER SERVING

		Daily Values
Calories	131	6%
Total fat	4 g	5%
Saturated fat	1 g	6%
Cholesterol	47 mg	15%
Sodium	162 mg	6%
Carbohydrate	5 g	1%
Fiber	1 g	2%
Protein	19 g	

P-s-s-s-s-t: Spray Secrets

Nonstick spray coating bypasses the mess of greasing pans. Even better, it contains only 0.8 gram of fat in a 1¼-second spray.

The "Secret" Ingredients
What is it about this spray that makes it so handy? Vegetable oils and lecithin (from soybeans) prevent the sticking, and alcohol aids the spray action but evaporates on contact. Aerosol-propellant cooking sprays rely on natural hydrocarbons rather than the chlorofluorocarbons that may be harmful to the ozone layer. Nonaerosol pump bottles also are available.

Handy Hints for Spray
● A 1¼-second spray replaces a tablespoon of butter, margarine, shortening, or cooking oil.
● Hold pans over your sink or trash can when spraying, so you don't make your floor or counter slippery.
● Spray only onto unheated baking pans or skillets. Cooking spray can flare up or smoke if sprayed onto a hot burner, gas flame, or hot pan.

● When using cooking spray instead of oil for stir-frying, cook over medium heat. High heat will cause the spray to smoke.
● Avoid spraying waffle irons. Buildup can cause foods to stick.
● Spray scissors before snipping dried fruit to prevent sticking.
● Ease cleanup by spraying your barbecue grill rack before using.
● Keep pasta water from bubbling over by spraying the pan first.
● Spritz bread or popped popcorn with butter-flavored spray for a buttery flavor without all the calories.

CHICKEN WITH MUSHROOM SAUCE

For a colorful sauce, use half of a green and half of a red sweet pepper (pictured on page 37).

EXCHANGES
2 STARCH
2 VERY LEAN MEAT
1 VEGETABLE

NUTRITION FACTS PER SERVING

		Daily Values
Calories	259	12%
Total fat	4 g	6%
Saturated fat	1 g	4%
Cholesterol	45 mg	14%
Sodium	176 mg	7%
Carbohydrate	32 g	10%
Fiber	1 g	2%
Protein	22 g	

4 small skinless, boneless chicken breast halves (about 12 ounces total)
Nonstick spray coating
1 teaspoon olive oil
2 cups sliced fresh mushrooms
1 medium red or green sweet pepper, cut into ¾-inch squares
1 clove garlic, minced
½ cup reduced-sodium chicken broth
½ cup fat-free dairy sour cream
1 tablespoon all-purpose flour
⅛ teaspoon black pepper
1 tablespoon dry sherry (optional)
2 cups hot cooked white or brown rice
Chives (optional)
Edible flowers (optional)

1. Rinse chicken; pat dry with paper towels. Spray an unheated large nonstick skillet with nonstick coating. Cook chicken over medium heat about 4 minutes or until browned, turning once. Remove chicken from skillet.

2. Carefully add olive oil to hot skillet. Cook mushrooms, sweet pepper, and garlic in hot oil until tender. Remove vegetables from skillet; cover with foil to keep warm. Carefully stir chicken broth into skillet. Return chicken breasts to skillet. Sprinkle chicken lightly with *salt* and *black pepper*. Bring to boiling. Reduce heat. Cover and simmer for 5 to 7 minutes or until chicken is tender and no longer pink. Transfer chicken to a serving platter; cover with foil to keep warm.

3. For sauce, in a small mixing bowl stir or whisk together sour cream, flour, and ⅛ teaspoon black pepper until smooth. If desired, stir in the sherry. Stir into mixture in skillet. Cook and stir until thickened and bubbly. Cook and stir for 1 minute more. Serve chicken, vegetables, and sauce over hot cooked rice. If desired, garnish with chives and flowers.

SPINACH CHICKEN WITH DIJON SAUCE

A spinach and cottage cheese stuffing fills these succulent chicken breasts, and a glistening mustard sauce adds the finishing touch.

EXCHANGES
3½ VERY LEAN MEAT
1 VEGETABLE

NUTRITION FACTS PER SERVING

		Daily Values
Calories	154	7%
Total fat	4 g	5%
Saturated fat	1 g	5%
Cholesterol	60 mg	20%
Sodium	302 mg	12%
Carbohydrate	4 g	1%
Fiber	0 g	0%
Protein	25 g	

1 cup reduced-sodium chicken broth
2½ teaspoons cornstarch
2 teaspoons coarse-grain brown mustard or honey mustard
1 egg white
½ of a 10-ounce package frozen chopped spinach, thawed and well-drained
¼ cup low-fat cottage cheese
2 tablespoons fine dry bread crumbs
⅛ teaspoon garlic salt
Dash ground nutmeg
6 medium skinless, boneless chicken breast halves (about 1½ pounds total)

1. For sauce, in a small saucepan stir together broth, cornstarch, and mustard. Set aside.

2. For stuffing, in a small mixing bowl lightly beat the egg white. Stir in the well-drained spinach, cottage cheese, bread crumbs, garlic salt, and nutmeg. Set aside.

3. Rinse chicken; pat dry with paper towels. Cut a pocket in each chicken breast half by cutting a horizontal slit through the thickest portion, cutting to but not through the opposite side. Spoon one-sixth of the stuffing into the pocket of each chicken breast. If necessary, secure with wooden toothpicks.

4. Place chicken on the unheated rack of a broiler pan. Broil 4 to 5 inches from the heat for 13 to 15 minutes or until chicken is tender and no longer pink, turning once. Meanwhile, cook and stir sauce until thickened and bubbly. Cook and stir for 2 minutes more. Serve the sauce with the chicken.

CITRUS CHICKEN SANDWICHES

MAKES 4 SERVINGS   PREP: 10 MINUTES   MARINATE: 4 TO 24 HOURS   BROIL: 12 MINUTES

Orange juice and mustard boost the flavor in this fat-free marinade.

EXCHANGES

2 STARCH
3 VERY LEAN MEAT
½ FRUIT
½ FAT

NUTRITION FACTS PER SERVING

		Daily Values
Calories	324	16%
Total fat	6 g	8%
Saturated fat	1 g	6%
Cholesterol	59 mg	19%
Sodium	574 mg	23%
Carbohydrate	38 g	12%
Fiber	1 g	2%
Protein	28 g	

4 medium skinless, boneless chicken breast halves (about 1 pound total)
¼ cup frozen orange juice concentrate, thawed
1 teaspoon prepared or Dijon-style mustard
2 cloves garlic, minced
¼ cup fat-free or light mayonnaise dressing or salad dressing
Dash ground ginger or 1 teaspoon frozen orange juice concentrate, thawed
4 kaiser rolls, split and toasted
1 cup alfalfa sprouts
4 lettuce leaves
4 tomato slices

1. Rinse chicken. Place chicken in a plastic bag set in a deep bowl. For marinade, stir together the ¼ cup orange juice concentrate, mustard, and garlic. Pour marinade over chicken. Close bag. Marinate in the refrigerator for 4 to 24 hours, turning bag occasionally. Drain chicken, discarding marinade.

2. Place chicken on the unheated rack of a broiler pan. Broil 4 to 5 inches from the heat for 12 to 15 minutes or until chicken is tender and no longer pink, turning once. (Or, grill on an uncovered grill directly over medium coals for 12 to 15 minutes or until chicken is tender and no longer pink, turning once.)

3. Meanwhile, stir together the mayonnaise dressing and the ginger or 1 teaspoon orange juice concentrate. Spread mayonnaise mixture on the cut sides of kaiser rolls. Layer bottom halves of the rolls with alfalfa sprouts, chicken, lettuce, and tomato. Add bun tops. Serve immediately.

JAMAICAN CHICKEN SALAD

MAKES 4 SERVINGS   PREP: 25 MINUTES

Jamaican jerk seasoning, a zesty mix of herbs and spices, enhances chicken and pork. Look for it with the other spices in your grocery store.

EXCHANGES

3 VERY LEAN MEAT
2 VEGETABLE
2 FRUIT
½ FAT

NUTRITION FACTS PER SERVING

		Daily Values
Calories	318	16%
Total fat	6 g	9%
Saturated fat	1 g	5%
Cholesterol	45 mg	15%
Sodium	572 mg	24%
Carbohydrate	35 g	12%
Fiber	4 g	16%
Protein	22 g	

½ cup bottled fat-free honey-mustard salad dressing
1 teaspoon finely shredded lime peel
4 medium skinless, boneless chicken breast halves (about 1 pound total)
2 to 3 teaspoons purchased or homemade Jamaican jerk seasoning*
2 teaspoons cooking oil
12 cups packaged torn mixed greens (such as European blend) (16 ounces)
16 chilled mango slices in light syrup, drained, or 2 large fresh mangoes, peeled, pitted, and sliced
Lime peel strips (optional)

1. For dressing, mix honey-mustard dressing and shredded lime peel. If necessary, add *water* to make of drizzling consistency. Cover and refrigerate until ready to serve.

2. Rinse chicken; pat dry with paper towels. Sprinkle chicken with the Jamaican jerk seasoning. In a 10-inch skillet cook the seasoned chicken in hot oil over medium-high heat about 12 minutes or until chicken is tender and no longer pink, turning once. Thinly bias-slice chicken.

3. Divide greens among 4 dinner plates. Arrange warm chicken and mango slices over greens; drizzle with dressing. If desired, top with strips of lime peel.

*Note: For homemade Jamaican jerk seasoning, combine 2 teaspoons *onion powder*, 1 teaspoon *sugar*, 1 teaspoon *crushed red pepper*, 1 teaspoon crushed *dried thyme*, ½ teaspoon *salt*, ½ teaspoon *ground cloves*, and ½ teaspoon *ground cinnamon*. Store the mixture in a covered container.

HOT TURKEY SUB SANDWICHES

MAKES 4 SERVINGS   PREP: 15 MINUTES   BAKE: 18 MINUTES

2 teaspoons olive oil
1 teaspoon dried basil, crushed
1 clove garlic, minced
1 8- or 9-ounce loaf or ½ of a
    16-ounce loaf unsliced
    French bread
3 ounces sliced cooked turkey
    breast
½ of a small cucumber, thinly
    sliced (about ½ cup)
3 ounces sliced mozzarella cheese
1 medium tomato, thinly sliced
⅛ teaspoon coarsely ground
    pepper

1. In a small mixing bowl or custard cup stir together the olive oil, basil, and garlic. Split the French bread lengthwise. Use a spoon to hollow out the bottom half, leaving a ¾-inch shell. Brush the cut surface of the top half with the olive oil mixture.

2. On the bottom half of the French bread, layer the turkey slices, cucumber, cheese, and tomato. Sprinkle with the pepper. Cover with the bread top. Serve sandwich immediately or wrap sandwich in foil and bake in a 375° oven for 18 to 20 minutes or until heated through. Cut crosswise into 4 portions.

If you have fresh basil growing in your garden or on your windowsill, omit the dried basil and layer a few fresh basil leaves on the sandwich.

EXCHANGES
2 STARCH
1½ LEAN MEAT
1 VEGETABLE
½ FAT

NUTRITION FACTS PER SERVING

		Daily Values
Calories	289	14%
Total fat	8 g	12%
Saturated fat	3 g	14%
Cholesterol	30 mg	9%
Sodium	501 mg	20%
Carbohydrate	36 g	11%
Fiber	1 g	2%
Protein	18 g	

Smart Sandwiches

Sandwiches are not only quick and easy to prepare, but they also can be a healthy part of anyone's diet. So start stacking, keeping the following healthy tips in mind.

Use whole grain bread or rolls for increased fiber. Choose bread or rolls that list whole wheat flour (or another whole grain flour) as the first ingredient.

Take control of the amount of fat and sodium in your sandwich meat by cooking and thinly slicing your own meat instead of using processed luncheon meats. A good choice is to roast a 2½- to 3-pound skinless turkey breast half with bone in a 325° oven for 2½ to 3 hours or until a meat thermometer registers 165°.

Eliminate fat-laden mayonnaise, margarine, and butter. Spread full-flavored mustard, fat-free mayonnaise dressing, or fat-free salad dressing on your bread.

Check out the dairy case to find the growing selection of reduced-fat and fat-free cheeses. Use these instead of their higher fat cousins.

Don't forget the fresh vegetables and fruit. Leaf lettuce, red and green sweet peppers, red onion, alfalfa sprouts, cucumbers, tomatoes, apples, pears, and shredded carrot all add fiber and vitamins as well as color, texture, and flavor to your sandwiches.

GARDEN TURKEY BURGERS

MAKES 6 SERVINGS   PREP: 30 MINUTES   GRILL: 15 MINUTES

All ground turkey is not equal. Select the leanest available or ask your butcher to grind skinless turkey breast.

EXCHANGES

| 2 STARCH |
| 2 MEDIUM-FAT MEAT |

NUTRITION FACTS PER SERVING

		Daily Values
Calories	285	14%
Total fat	11 g	17%
Saturated fat	2 g	11%
Cholesterol	28 mg	9%
Sodium	464 mg	19%
Carbohydrate	32 g	10%
Fiber	4 g	16%
Protein	16 g	

½ cup shredded carrot
½ cup shredded zucchini
¼ cup reduced-calorie cucumber ranch or creamy cucumber salad dressing
2 green onions, sliced
1 clove garlic, minced
2 teaspoons snipped fresh oregano or basil, or ½ teaspoon dried oregano or basil, crushed
⅛ teaspoon salt
⅛ teaspoon pepper
¾ cup quick-cooking rolled oats
1 pound lean ground raw turkey
Nonstick spray coating
3 tablespoons reduced-calorie cucumber ranch or creamy cucumber salad dressing
6 whole wheat hamburger buns, split and toasted
6 lettuce leaves
6 thin tomato slices

1. In a small mixing bowl stir together the carrot, zucchini, the ¼ cup salad dressing, the green onions, garlic, oregano, salt, and pepper. Stir in oats. Add turkey; mix well. Shape into six ¾-inch-thick patties.

2. Spray an unheated wire grill basket with nonstick coating. Place burgers in grill basket. Grill on an uncovered grill directly over medium-hot coals for 15 to 18 minutes or until burgers are no longer pink, turning once. Spread the 3 tablespoons salad dressing on cut sides of the buns. Serve burgers in buns with lettuce and tomato slices.

ORANGE BARBECUED TURKEY

MAKES 4 SERVINGS   PREP: 15 MINUTES   MARINATE: 30 MINUTES   GRILL: 12 MINUTES

Turkey tops the list of convenience meats. The marinade—using readily available ingredients—makes it an even easier meal.

EXCHANGES

| 3 VERY LEAN MEAT |
| ½ FRUIT |
| ½ FAT |

NUTRITION FACTS PER SERVING

		Daily Values
Calories	162	8%
Total fat	6 g	9%
Saturated fat	1 g	5%
Cholesterol	50 mg	17%
Sodium	206 mg	9%
Carbohydrate	4 g	1%
Fiber	0 g	0%
Protein	22 g	

1 teaspoon finely shredded orange peel
½ cup orange juice
1 tablespoon cooking oil
2 teaspoons Worcestershire sauce
1 teaspoon dry mustard
½ teaspoon lemon-pepper seasoning
⅛ teaspoon garlic powder
4 turkey breast tenderloin steaks, cut ¼ to ½ inch thick (about 1 pound total)

1. For the marinade, combine the orange peel, orange juice, cooking oil, Worcestershire sauce, dry mustard, lemon-pepper seasoning, and garlic powder.

2. Rinse turkey steaks; pat dry with paper towels. Place the steaks in a shallow pan. Pour the marinade over the steaks. Turn steaks to coat with marinade. Let stand at room temperature about 30 minutes.

3. Drain steaks well, reserving the marinade. Grill steaks on an uncovered grill directly over medium coals for 12 to 15 minutes or until turkey is tender and no longer pink, turning once and brushing frequently with marinade.

FRESH TOMATO AND TURKEY PIZZA

MAKES 4 SERVINGS   PREP: 10 MINUTES   BAKE: 13 MINUTES

Nonstick spray coating
1 tablespoon cornmeal
1 10-ounce package refrigerated pizza dough
3 medium plum tomatoes, thinly sliced
4 ounces cooked turkey breast or smoked turkey breast, cut into thin strips
3 tablespoons snipped fresh basil
¼ teaspoon coarsely ground pepper
1 cup shredded reduced-fat mozzarella cheese (4 ounces)

1. Spray a 12-inch pizza pan with nonstick coating. Sprinkle cornmeal in bottom of pizza pan. Press refrigerated dough into prepared pan, building up edges.

2. Arrange tomato slices and turkey strips on the dough. Sprinkle with fresh basil and pepper. Sprinkle mozzarella cheese over all. Bake in a 425° oven for 13 to 18 minutes or until cheese bubbles.

This pizza goes together with ease. Start with refrigerated pizza dough and top it off with fresh tomato slices, deli turkey, and packaged shredded mozzarella cheese.

EXCHANGES

| 2 STARCH |
| 2 LEAN MEAT |
| ½ VEGETABLE |

NUTRITION FACTS PER SERVING

		Daily Values
Calories	288	14%
Total fat	8 g	11%
Saturated fat	4 g	17%
Cholesterol	39 mg	12%
Sodium	449 mg	18%
Carbohydrate	32 g	10%
Fiber	2 g	8%
Protein	21 g	

TURKEY TENDERLOINS IN PAPRIKA SAUCE

MAKES 4 SERVINGS   PREP: 15 MINUTES

2 tablespoons lemon juice
1 clove garlic, minced
¼ teaspoon pepper
4 turkey breast tenderloin steaks or 2 whole turkey breast tenderloins (about 1 pound total)
Nonstick spray coating
½ of a 14½-ounce can low-sodium tomatoes, cut up
¼ cup light dairy sour cream
1 tablespoon dry sherry (optional)
1 teaspoon paprika
Nonstick spray coating
1 cup sliced fresh mushrooms
2 tablespoons snipped fresh parsley
2 cups hot cooked rice

1. In a small bowl combine lemon juice, garlic, and pepper. Rinse turkey; pat dry with paper towels. If using whole turkey tenderloins, halve them lengthwise to make 4 tenderloin steaks, each about ½ inch thick. Spray the unheated rack of a broiler pan with nonstick coating. Arrange turkey steaks on broiler pan. Brush with half of the lemon juice mixture.

2. Broil 4 inches from the heat for 6 to 8 minutes or until turkey is tender and no longer pink, turning and brushing with the remaining lemon juice mixture once.

3. For sauce, in a blender container combine tomatoes, sour cream, sherry (if desired), and paprika. Cover and blend until smooth. Spray an unheated medium nonstick skillet with nonstick coating. Cook mushrooms in the skillet for 3 minutes. Add tomato mixture; heat through, but *do not* boil. Stir in parsley. Serve turkey over hot cooked rice. Spoon sauce over all.

This saucy turkey dish tastes much like a classic chicken paprikash, but is lower in fat and calories and is ready in about half the time.

EXCHANGES

| 1 STARCH |
| 3 VERY LEAN MEAT |
| 2 VEGETABLE |

NUTRITION FACTS PER SERVING

		Daily Values
Calories	254	13%
Total fat	4 g	6%
Saturated fat	1 g	5%
Cholesterol	54 mg	18%
Sodium	66 mg	3%
Carbohydrate	27 g	9%
Fiber	1 g	4%
Protein	25 g	

HOT ORIENTAL BEEF AND PASTA

MAKES 4 SERVINGS   PREP: 25 MINUTES   COOK: 15 MINUTES

12 ounces boneless beef top sirloin steak, cut 1 inch thick
4 ounces packaged dried spaghetti or vermicelli, broken, or rotini
¼ cup orange juice
2 tablespoons hoisin sauce
1 tablespoon reduced-sodium soy sauce
½ teaspoon toasted sesame oil
⅛ teaspoon ground red pepper
   Nonstick spray coating
1 clove garlic, minced
10 ounces fresh asparagus, cut into 1-inch pieces (about 2 cups)
1 medium carrot, cut into thin strips
1 small red onion, cut into wedges

1. Trim fat from beef. Partially freeze beef. Thinly slice across the grain into bite-size strips. Set aside.

2. Cook pasta according to package directions, except omit any oil and salt. Drain pasta. Cover and keep warm.

3. Meanwhile, for sauce, stir together orange juice, hoisin sauce, soy sauce, sesame oil, and red pepper. Set aside.

4. Spray an unheated wok or 12-inch skillet with nonstick coating. Preheat over medium-high heat until a drop of water sizzles. Add garlic; stir-fry for 15 seconds. Add asparagus and carrot; stir-fry for 1 minute. Add onion; stir-fry for 2 to 3 minutes more or until vegetables are crisp-tender. Remove vegetables from wok or skillet.

5. Add beef to wok or skillet. Stir-fry about 3 minutes or until desired doneness. Return vegetables to wok or skillet. Drizzle sauce over all. Toss to coat all ingredients. Heat through. Serve over pasta.

Hoisin sauce, a condiment made of soybeans, garlic, chili peppers, and various spices, is also called Peking sauce. (Beef pictured on page 42.)

EXCHANGES

| 2 STARCH |
| 2½ LEAN MEAT |
| 1 VEGETABLE |

NUTRITION FACTS PER SERVING

		Daily Values
Calories	331	16%
Total fat	9 g	14%
Saturated fat	3 g	16%
Cholesterol	57 mg	18%
Sodium	353 mg	14%
Carbohydrate	35 g	11%
Fiber	2 g	8%
Protein	26 g	

Measuring Dry and Cooked Pasta

*I*f you don't have a kitchen scale, be aware of the following cup measurements for pasta.

Four ounces of uncooked elbow macaroni or medium shell macaroni measures about 1 cup. When it's cooked, you'll have approximately 2½ cups pasta.

Four ounces of uncooked medium noodles measure about 3 cups. Noodles will measure the same when they're cooked.

Four ounces of uncooked 10-inch-long spaghetti, held together in a bunch, has about a 1-inch diameter. When it's cooked, you'll have about 2 cups of pasta.

Hearty Beef Stew

MAKES 6 SERVINGS   PREP: 30 MINUTES   COOK: CROCKERY COOKER 5–12 HOURS; RANGE TOP 1½ HOURS

For just 4 grams of fat and 263 calories, you get a hearty beef stew that's filled with potatoes and vegetables. Serve it with wedges of crusty French bread.

EXCHANGES

1½ STARCH	
2 LEAN MEAT	
2 VEGETABLE	

NUTRITION FACTS PER SERVING

		Daily Values
Calories	263	13%
Total fat	4 g	6%
Saturated fat	1 g	6%
Cholesterol	48 mg	15%
Sodium	413 mg	17%
Carbohydrate	35 g	11%
Fiber	3 g	12%
Protein	22 g	

1 pound beef round steak
  Nonstick spray coating
3 medium potatoes, cut into ¾-inch pieces
3 medium carrots, cut into ½-inch pieces
1 medium onion, cut into thin wedges
1 9-ounce package frozen cut green beans
3 tablespoons quick-cooking tapioca
1 teaspoon dried thyme, crushed
1 teaspoon dried basil, crushed
1 teaspoon instant beef bouillon granules
1 teaspoon sugar
½ teaspoon salt
¼ teaspoon pepper
2 cups water
1 14½-ounce can low-sodium tomatoes, cut up
1 8-ounce can low-sodium tomato sauce

1. Trim fat from meat. Cut meat into ½-inch cubes. Spray an unheated large nonstick skillet with nonstick coating. In skillet quickly brown meat, half at a time. Drain well.

2. Meanwhile, in a 3½- or 4-quart crockery cooker combine potatoes, carrots, and onion. Add frozen green beans, tapioca, thyme, basil, bouillon, sugar, salt, and pepper. Stir in browned meat, water, *undrained* tomatoes, and tomato sauce.

3. Cover; cook on low-heat setting for 10 to 12 hours or on high-heat setting for 5 to 6 hours.

Range-top directions: Spray an unheated large nonstick saucepan with nonstick coating. In the saucepan quickly brown the meat, half at a time. Drain well. Return all meat to saucepan. Stir in tapioca, thyme, basil, bouillon granules, sugar, salt, pepper, water, *undrained* tomatoes, and tomato sauce. Bring to boiling; reduce heat. Simmer, covered, about 1 hour or until meat is nearly tender, stirring occasionally. Stir in potatoes, carrots, onion, and green beans. Return to boiling; reduce heat. Simmer, covered, for 30 minutes or until vegetables are tender.

To Peel or Not to Peel

To make a dish more nutritious, you can omit peeling many fruits and vegetables, such as potatoes, tomatoes, carrots, parsnips, pears, apples, and nectarines. You'll be increasing the fiber content since much of the fiber in fruits and vegetables is contained in the peels. Before cutting up unpeeled fruits and vegetables, scrub them thoroughly with a soft vegetable brush until clean. Do not use soap. Not peeling also makes the dish faster and easier to prepare.

LEMON PEPPER STEAK

MAKES 4 SERVINGS   PREP: 10 MINUTES   BROIL: 10 MINUTES

2 beef top loin steaks, cut 1 inch
  thick (about 1 pound total)
1 teaspoon olive oil or cooking oil
2 cloves garlic, minced
1 tablespoon snipped fresh
  oregano or 1 teaspoon dried
  oregano, crushed
1 teaspoon finely shredded
  lemon peel
¼ teaspoon coarsely ground
  pepper

1. Trim fat from steaks. In a small mixing bowl stir together oil, garlic, oregano, lemon peel, and pepper. Using your fingers, rub onto both sides of steaks.

2. Place steaks on the unheated rack of a broiler pan. Broil 3 inches from the heat until desired doneness, turning once. Allow 10 to 12 minutes for medium-rare or 13 to 17 minutes for medium. (Or, grill steaks on an uncovered grill directly over medium-hot coals until desired doneness, turning once. Allow 10 to 12 minutes for medium-rare or 12 to 15 minutes for medium.) To serve, thinly slice steak into strips.

Half a steak provides plenty of protein for one person. Round out the meal with lots of fruits and vegetables.

EXCHANGES
3½ LEAN MEAT

NUTRITION FACTS PER SERVING		
		Daily Values
Calories	215	10%
Total fat	11 g	17%
Saturated fat	4 g	21%
Cholesterol	76 mg	25%
Sodium	56 mg	2%
Carbohydrate	1 g	0%
Fiber	0 g	0%
Protein	26 g	

STEAK WITH MARSALA SAUCE

MAKES 4 SERVINGS   PREP: 10 MINUTES   COOK: 10 MINUTES

12 ounces boneless beef sirloin
  steak, cut 1 inch thick
  Nonstick spray coating
2 cups sliced fresh mushrooms
1 medium onion, sliced and
  separated into rings
⅓ cup dry Marsala or apple juice
¼ cup water
2 tablespoons snipped fresh
  parsley
½ teaspoon instant beef bouillon
  granules
⅛ teaspoon pepper
  Hot cooked noodles (optional)

1. Trim fat from steak. Place steak on the unheated rack of a broiler pan. Broil 4 to 5 inches from the heat until desired doneness, turning once. Allow 10 to 12 minutes for medium-rare or 13 to 17 minutes for medium.

2. Meanwhile, for sauce, spray an unheated large skillet with nonstick coating. Cook mushrooms and onion in skillet over medium heat until tender. Stir in Marsala or apple juice, water, parsley, bouillon granules, and pepper. Bring to boiling. Boil gently, uncovered, about 6 minutes or until liquid is nearly evaporated.

3. To serve, thinly slice steak. Serve steak with sauce. If desired, serve over hot cooked noodles.

Marsala, originally from Sicily, adds a rich flavor to the mushroom sauce that tops this broiled or grilled steak.

EXCHANGES
2½ LEAN MEAT
1 VEGETABLE

NUTRITION FACTS PER SERVING		
		Daily Values
Calories	183	9%
Total fat	8 g	12%
Saturated fat	3 g	15%
Cholesterol	57 mg	18%
Sodium	154 mg	6%
Carbohydrate	4 g	1%
Fiber	1 g	3%
Protein	20 g	

CITRUS-TEQUILA FAJITAS

MAKES 4 SERVINGS   PREP: 10 MINUTES   MARINATE: 30 MINUTES TO 4 HOURS   BROIL: 12 MINUTES

12 ounces beef flank steak
 3 tablespoons frozen orange juice
   concentrate, thawed
 3 tablespoons tequila or water
 2 tablespoons lime juice
 1 teaspoon grated gingerroot
 ½ teaspoon dried oregano,
   crushed
 ⅛ teaspoon salt
 ⅛ teaspoon ground red pepper
 1 clove garlic, minced
 8 small corn or four 8- to
   10-inch flour tortillas
 ½ of a red or yellow sweet pepper,
   cut into strips
 ½ of a small onion, sliced and
   separated into rings
   Sliced fresh chili peppers
   (optional)

1. Score meat by making shallow cuts at 1-inch intervals diagonally across steak in a diamond pattern. Repeat on the other side. Place meat in a plastic bag set in a shallow dish. For marinade, stir together orange juice concentrate, tequila or water, lime juice, gingerroot, oregano, salt, ground red pepper, and garlic. Pour over meat in bag. Close bag. Marinate 30 minutes at room temperature or in the refrigerator up to 4 hours, turning bag occasionally.

2. Drain meat, reserving marinade. Place meat on the unheated rack of a broiler pan. Broil meat 3 inches from the heat for 12 to 14 minutes or until desired doneness, turning once. (Or, grill meat on an uncovered grill directly over medium coals for 12 to 14 minutes or until desired doneness, turning once.) Thinly slice meat diagonally across the grain.

3. To warm tortillas, wrap in foil. Place beside broiler pan or on grill rack for the last 8 minutes of cooking meat.

4. Meanwhile, pour reserved marinade into a small saucepan. Stir in sweet pepper strips and onion. Bring to boiling; reduce heat. Simmer, uncovered, for 3 to 5 minutes or until vegetables are tender.

5. To serve, immediately fill warmed tortillas with beef. Using a slotted spoon, spoon pepper-onion mixture over beef. If desired, sprinkle with chili peppers. Roll up fajitas.

Scoring and marinating tenderizes flank steak, a naturally lean cut of meat, without chemical tenderizers. (Fajitas pictured on page 46.)

EXCHANGES

1 STARCH	
2 LEAN MEAT	
1 VEGETABLE	
½ FRUIT	

NUTRITION FACTS PER SERVING

		Daily Values
Calories	282	14%
Total fat	8 g	12%
Saturated fat	3 g	15%
Cholesterol	40 mg	13%
Sodium	179 mg	7%
Carbohydrate	30 g	10%
Fiber	0 g	0%
Protein	20 g	

Using Fresh Ginger

When you're looking for ways to add a new twist of flavor to a favorite recipe, try gingerroot. It's great in stir-fries, salads, vegetable dishes, and baked goods. It's simple to store and easy to use.
■ Choose plump, firm gingerroot with light, shiny skins that have no soft spots or wrinkles.
■ Wrap the whole gingerroot in paper towels and store for up to 1 month in the refrigerator.
■ Wrap cut ginger in plastic wrap. Keep in the refrigerator for several weeks. Or, place the cut-up ginger in a small jar. Fill the jar with dry sherry or wine; cover and refrigerate for up to 3 months. (Use the ginger-infused liquid in stir-fries or toss with cooked vegetables.)
■ Freeze whole or grated gingerroot for up to 3 months. Thawing makes it soft but still suitable for cooking.
■ Leave the skin on gingerroot until you're ready to use it. Trim the skin from only the portion you need.
■ Grate or mince gingerroot to use in stir-fries, salad dressings, marinades, sauces, and baked foods. Discard the stringy fibers left on the root.

■ A 2×1-inch piece of gingerroot yields about 2 tablespoons of grated ginger.
■ Chop or cut gingerroot into slivers for a more intense ginger flavor.
■ Slice ginger and add to soups, broths, cooking liquids, and beverages, such as tea. Remove the slice before serving.
■ If you're short on fresh ginger, substitute ¼ teaspoon ground ginger for each teaspoon of grated fresh gingerroot called for in a recipe.
■ Fresh ginger contains an enzyme that breaks down proteins, so it works well in marinades to tenderize meats.

Pork with Apple-Sour Cream Sauce

MAKES 4 SERVINGS   PREP: 10 MINUTES   COOK: 20 MINUTES

Apple slices and a hint of sage complement these medaillons of pork (pictured on page 49). Apple juice adds a light sweetness.

Exchanges

| 2 Starch |
| 2½ Very Lean Meat |
| 1 Fruit |
| ½ Milk |

Nutrition Facts Per Serving

		Daily Values
Calories	373	18%
Total fat	4 g	6%
Saturated fat	1 g	5%
Cholesterol	60 mg	20%
Sodium	231 mg	10%
Carbohydrate	54 g	18%
Fiber	1 g	4%
Protein	28 g	

12 ounces pork tenderloin
  Nonstick spray coating
1 medium apple, cored and thinly sliced
¾ cup apple juice or apple cider
1 small onion, chopped
¼ teaspoon salt
¼ teaspoon dried sage, crushed
1 8-ounce carton fat-free dairy sour cream
2 tablespoons all-purpose flour
1 9-ounce package refrigerated spinach fettuccine or 4 ounces packaged dried spinach fettuccine, cooked and drained
  Cracked black pepper (optional)

1. Trim fat from pork. Cut pork crosswise into 4 slices. Place each slice of pork, cut side down, between 2 sheets of plastic wrap. Lightly pound meat with the flat side of a meat mallet to ½-inch thickness.

2. Spray an unheated large skillet with nonstick coating. Preheat the skillet over medium heat. Cook the pork slices, half at a time, in the skillet over medium-high heat for 3½ to 4 minutes or until pork is slightly pink in center and juices run clear, turning once. Remove pork from skillet. Keep warm.

3. For sauce, add apple slices, apple juice, onion, salt, and sage to skillet. Bring just to boiling; reduce heat. Simmer, covered, for 4 to 5 minutes or until apple is just tender. Using a slotted spoon, carefully remove apple slices and set aside. In a small bowl stir together sour cream and flour. Add sour cream mixture to skillet. Cook and stir until thickened and bubbly. Cook and stir for 1 minute more. Arrange pork and apple slices over fettuccine. Spoon sauce over pork, apple slices, and pasta. If desired, sprinkle with pepper.

Orange-Glazed Pork Chops

MAKES 4 SERVINGS   PREP: 12 MINUTES   BROIL: 12 MINUTES

Just a few ingredients take pork chops from an ordinary meal to company-special.

Exchanges

| 2 Lean Meat |
| ½ Fruit |

Nutrition Facts Per Serving

		Daily Values
Calories	109	5%
Total fat	4 g	6%
Saturated fat	1 g	5%
Cholesterol	29 mg	10%
Sodium	253 mg	11%
Carbohydrate	8 g	3%
Fiber	0 g	0%
Protein	10 g	

1 tablespoon brown sugar
1 teaspoon cornstarch
½ teaspoon finely shredded orange peel
½ teaspoon grated gingerroot
⅛ teaspoon ground red pepper
½ cup orange juice
1 tablespoon soy sauce
4 pork loin chops, cut ¾ inch thick (about 1½ pounds total)

1. For glaze, in a saucepan stir together brown sugar, cornstarch, orange peel, gingerroot, and red pepper. Stir in orange juice and soy sauce. Cook and stir until thickened and bubbly. Cook and stir for 2 minutes more. Keep glaze warm.

2. Trim the excess fat from the chops. Place the chops on the unheated rack of a broiler pan. Broil 3 to 4 inches from the heat for 12 to 14 minutes or until pork is slightly pink in center and the juices run clear, turning once. Brush the chops with the glaze during the last 5 minutes of broiling. Pass remaining glaze.

HAM AND BROCCOLI SOUFFLÉ

MAKES 4 SERVINGS   PREP: 30 MINUTES   BAKE: 45 MINUTES

Healthful diets can include 3 to 4 egg yolks per week. This recipe contains only half a yolk per serving.

EXCHANGES

1 STARCH	
2 LEAN MEAT	
½ VEGETABLE	

NUTRITION FACTS PER SERVING

		Daily Values
Calories	197	9%
Total fat	7 g	10%
Saturated fat	3 g	13%
Cholesterol	129 mg	42%
Sodium	452 mg	18%
Carbohydrate	15 g	5%
Fiber	2 g	9%
Protein	18 g	

Nonstick spray coating
2 tablespoons cornmeal or fine dry bread crumbs
1½ cups broccoli flowerets
Nonstick spray coating
2 green onions, sliced
¾ cup skim milk
¼ cup all-purpose flour
⅛ teaspoon ground red pepper
½ cup shredded reduced-fat sharp cheddar cheese (2 ounces)
2 beaten egg yolks
3 ounces cooked ham, finely chopped (½ cup)
4 egg whites
¼ teaspoon cream of tartar

1. Spray a 1½-quart soufflé dish with nonstick coating. Sprinkle with cornmeal or dry bread crumbs. Set aside.

2. Cut broccoli flowerets into ½-inch pieces. Place broccoli in the top of a steamer over *boiling water*. Cover and steam for 3 to 5 minutes or until crisp-tender. Remove from steamer. Set aside.

3. Spray an unheated medium saucepan with nonstick coating. Cook green onions in saucepan over medium heat until tender. In a screw-top jar combine milk, flour, and red pepper. Shake to combine. Stir into green onions in saucepan. Cook and stir until thickened and bubbly. Remove from heat (mixture will be thick). Stir in cheese until melted. Stir about half of the cheese sauce into the beaten egg yolks. Return all to the saucepan. Stir in chopped ham and steamed broccoli.

4. In a large mixing bowl beat egg whites and cream of tartar with an electric mixer on medium to high speed until stiff peaks form (tips stand straight). Gently fold about 1 cup of the egg whites into the cheese mixture.

5. Gradually pour cheese mixture over remaining beaten egg whites, folding to combine. Pour into the prepared soufflé dish. Bake in a 350° oven about 45 minutes or until a knife inserted near center comes out clean. Serve immediately.

Natural and Process Cheese

Cheese made directly from the curd of milk and not reprocessed or blended is known as natural cheese. Process cheese is made from natural cheese that has undergone additional steps, such as pasteurization. Process cheese often has other ingredients added to it for flavor, a softer texture, and longer shelf life.

To help hold the line on fat, look for lower-fat and fat-free natural and process cheeses. The following cheeses are used in the recipes for this book.

Reduced-fat natural cheese: A natural cheese, such as cheddar, Swiss, and Monterey Jack cheese, with fewer grams of fat than regular natural cheese. Lower-fat mozzarella is called "part-skim mozzarella cheese."

Reduced-fat flavored process cheese product: A lower-fat process cheese that is available in American, cheddar, and Swiss flavors.

Fat-free process cheese product: A process cheese without any fat.

HONEY HAM SALAD

MAKES 4 SERVINGS   PREP: 25 MINUTES

4 cups torn mixed greens
1 cup cauliflower flowerets
4 ounces lean cooked ham, cut
   into thin strips
½ cup shredded carrot
2 tablespoons sliced green onion
2 tablespoons golden raisins
3 tablespoons honey
½ teaspoon finely shredded lime
   peel
2 tablespoons lime juice
2 teaspoons olive oil
1 teaspoon Dijon-style mustard
   or prepared mustard

1. In a large salad bowl toss together greens, cauliflower, ham, carrot, green onion, and raisins.

2. For dressing, in a screw-top jar combine honey, lime peel, lime juice, olive oil, and mustard. Cover and shake until combined. Before serving, drizzle dressing over salad; toss to coat well.

Need to stretch your meat exchanges? This salad is the perfect answer. It's satisfying and filling, yet uses only 1 meat exchange.

EXCHANGES

| 1 LEAN MEAT |
| 2 VEGETABLE |
| ½ FRUIT |

NUTRITION FACTS PER SERVING

		Daily Values
Calories	151	7%
Total fat	4 g	6%
Saturated fat	1 g	4%
Cholesterol	15 mg	4%
Sodium	401 mg	16%
Carbohydrate	22 g	7%
Fiber	2 g	6%
Protein	8 g	

HAM AND BEAN SOUP

MAKES 4 SERVINGS   PREP: 20 MINUTES   SOAK: 1 HOUR OR OVERNIGHT   COOK: 1¼ HOURS

1 cup dry navy beans
1 cup sliced celery
1 cup sliced carrots
1 cup chopped onion
¾ cup chopped, cooked, lower-
   sodium ham
1 teaspoon instant chicken
   bouillon granules
1 teaspoon dried thyme, crushed
2 bay leaves
¼ teaspoon pepper

1. Rinse beans; drain. In a large saucepan combine the beans and 4 cups *water*. Bring to boiling; reduce heat. Simmer, uncovered, for 2 minutes. Remove from heat. Cover and let stand for 1 hour. (Or, soak the beans overnight in 4 cups *water* in a covered pan.) Drain and rinse beans.

2. In the same saucepan stir together the beans, 4 cups *fresh water*, celery, carrots, onion, ham, bouillon granules, thyme, bay leaves, and pepper. Bring to boiling; reduce heat. Simmer, covered, for 1¼ hours or until the beans are tender. Discard bay leaves. Using a fork, slightly mash the beans against a side of the saucepan to slightly thicken the soup.

Pair this old-fashioned soup with a loaf of crusty French bread and a salad.

EXCHANGES

| 2 STARCH |
| 1 VERY LEAN MEAT |
| 2 VEGETABLE |

NUTRITION FACTS PER SERVING

		Daily Values
Calories	247	12%
Total fat	2 g	3%
Saturated fat	0 g	0%
Cholesterol	12 mg	4%
Sodium	571 mg	4%
Carbohydrate	42 g	14%
Fiber	2 g	8%
Protein	17 g	

PORK AND FRUIT SALAD

MAKES 4 SERVINGS   PREP: 15 MINUTES   ROAST: 25 MINUTES   STAND: 5 MINUTES

¼ cup fat-free mayonnaise dressing or salad dressing
¼ cup unsweetened pineapple juice or orange juice
1 tablespoon honey mustard
½ teaspoon grated gingerroot
12 ounces pork tenderloin
2 tablespoons honey mustard
6 cups torn spinach and/or romaine
2 cups sliced pears, apples, nectarines, and/or peeled peaches
12 small clusters champagne grapes
   Coarsely ground pepper (optional)

1. For dressing, in a small mixing bowl stir together the mayonnaise dressing or salad dressing, pineapple or orange juice, the 1 tablespoon honey mustard, and the gingerroot. Cover and refrigerate until serving time.

2. Trim any fat from the tenderloin. Place in a shallow roasting pan. Insert a meat thermometer. Roast, uncovered, in a 425° oven for 20 minutes.

3. Spoon the 2 tablespoons honey mustard over the tenderloin. Roast for 5 to 10 minutes more or until thermometer registers 160°. Cover meat loosely with foil and let stand for 5 minutes before carving.

4. Meanwhile, arrange greens, fruit slices, and grapes on 4 salad plates. To serve, thinly slice pork roast. Top salads with pork slices. Stir dressing. Drizzle dressing over salads. If desired, sprinkle with pepper.

Pork tenderloin has only 4 grams of fat and 67 mg of cholesterol in a 3-ounce serving. That's similar to skinless chicken breast, which has 3 g fat and 72 mg cholesterol in a 3-ounce serving. (Salad pictured on page 52.)

EXCHANGES

2½ LEAN MEAT
1½ VEGETABLE
1 FRUIT

NUTRITION FACTS PER SERVING

		Daily Values
Calories	228	11%
Total fat	4 g	6%
Saturated fat	1 g	5%
Cholesterol	60 mg	20%
Sodium	442 mg	18%
Carbohydrate	27 g	9%
Fiber	5 g	18%
Protein	22 g	

Mayonnaise Options

Although fat-free mayonnaise may sound like the best choice when selecting mayonnaise, it may not be if you are concerned about sodium. The sodium often increases as the fat decreases. The chart below compares a tablespoon of mayonnaise, reduced-fat mayonnaise dressing, and fat-free mayonnaise dressing.

	Calories	Fat	Sodium
Mayonnaise	100	12 g	70 mg
Reduced-fat mayonnaise	50	5 g	110 mg
Fat-free mayonnaise dressing	12	0 g	190 mg

A good solution is to mix either reduced-fat mayonnaise or fat-free mayonnaise dressing with plain nonfat yogurt for a delicious tangy dressing. Nonfat yogurt has only 11 mg sodium per tablespoon.

GRILLED VEAL CHOPS

MAKES 4 SERVINGS   PREP: 10 MINUTES   MARINATE: 30 MINUTES   GRILL: 8 MINUTES

Red wine vinegar adds flavor without adding fat or many calories to this company-special entrée.

EXCHANGES
2 LEAN MEAT

NUTRITION FACTS PER SERVING

		Daily Values
Calories	113	6%
Total fat	4 g	6%
Saturated fat	1 g	5%
Cholesterol	55 mg	18%
Sodium	138 mg	6%
Carbohydrate	6 g	2%
Fiber	0 g	0%
Protein	14 g	

⅓ cup red wine vinegar
1 tablespoon honey
2 teaspoons Worcestershire sauce
2 teaspoons Dijon-style mustard
1½ teaspoons snipped fresh thyme
   or ½ teaspoon dried thyme, crushed
¼ teaspoon pepper
4 boneless veal loin chops or boneless pork loin chops (12 to 14 ounces total)

1. For marinade, in a small mixing bowl stir together vinegar, honey, Worcestershire sauce, mustard, thyme, and pepper. Place chops in a plastic bag set in a deep bowl. Pour marinade over meat. Close bag. Marinate at room temperature for 30 minutes, turning bag occasionally. Drain chops, reserving marinade.

2. Grill chops directly over medium-hot coals for 8 to 11 minutes or until veal or pork is slightly pink in center and juices run clear, turning once. (Or, place chops on the unheated rack of a broiler pan. Broil 4 to 5 inches from the heat for 10 to 12 minutes or until veal or pork is slightly pink in center and juices run clear, turning once.) Brush chops with reserved marinade up to the last 5 minutes of grilling or broiling.

VEAL PARMIGIANA

MAKES 4 SERVINGS   PREP: 30 MINUTES   BAKE: 6 MINUTES

There's no oil needed here. Oven-frying at a high temperature for a short time produces a crispy coating without added fat.

EXCHANGES
½ STARCH
3 LEAN MEAT
1 VEGETABLE

NUTRITION FACTS PER SERVING

		Daily Values
Calories	217	11%
Total fat	7 g	11%
Saturated fat	3 g	15%
Cholesterol	78 mg	26%
Sodium	290 mg	12%
Carbohydrate	11 g	4%
Fiber	1 g	4%
Protein	26 g	

12 ounces boneless veal leg sirloin steak or veal leg round steak, cut ½ inch thick
⅓ cup fine dry bread crumbs
2 tablespoons grated Parmesan cheese
¼ teaspoon dried Italian seasoning, crushed
1 slightly beaten egg white
1 tablespoon water
   Nonstick spray coating
1 8-ounce can low-sodium tomato sauce
½ teaspoon dried Italian seasoning, crushed
⅓ cup shredded reduced-fat mozzarella cheese (1½ ounces)
2 teaspoons grated Parmesan cheese

1. Cut veal into 4 serving-size pieces. Place each piece of veal between 2 pieces of plastic wrap. Working from the center to the edges, lightly pound the veal with the flat side of a meat mallet to ⅛-inch thickness. In a shallow dish stir together the bread crumbs, the 2 tablespoons Parmesan cheese, and the ¼ teaspoon Italian seasoning.

2. In another shallow dish stir together the egg white and water. Dip the veal pieces in the egg white mixture, then in the crumb mixture to coat. Spray a shallow baking pan with the nonstick coating. Place veal in pan. Bake in a 450° oven for 6 to 8 minutes or until veal is slightly pink in center and juices run clear.

3. Meanwhile, for sauce, in a small saucepan stir together the tomato sauce and the ½ teaspoon Italian seasoning. Bring to boiling; remove from heat. Spoon sauce over veal in pan. Top with mozzarella cheese and the 2 teaspoons Parmesan cheese. Bake veal for 2 minutes more or until the mozzarella cheese melts.

CURRIED LAMB

MAKES 4 SERVINGS   PREP: 25 MINUTES   COOK: 45 MINUTES

Nonstick spray coating
12 ounces boneless lean lamb, cut
     into 1-inch cubes
¾ cup chopped onion
1 to 2 teaspoons curry powder
1 clove garlic, minced
1 cup water
¾ cup apple juice or apple cider
3 stalks celery, bias-sliced into
     ½-inch pieces (1½ cups)
⅓ cup mixed dried fruit bits,
     raisins, or chopped dried
     apricots
½ teaspoon instant chicken
     bouillon granules
⅛ teaspoon pepper
2 tablespoons cold water
1 tablespoon cornstarch
2 cups hot cooked rice

1. Spray an unheated large saucepan with nonstick coating. Preheat over medium heat. Add the meat, onion, curry powder, and garlic to saucepan. Cook until meat is brown and onion is tender.

2. Stir in the 1 cup water and the apple juice. Add celery, dried fruit, bouillon granules, and pepper. Bring to boiling; reduce heat. Simmer, covered, for 45 to 60 minutes or until lamb is tender.

3. Stir together the 2 tablespoons cold water and the cornstarch. Stir into mixture in saucepan. Cook and stir until thickened and bubbly. Cook and stir for 2 minutes more. Serve over hot cooked rice.

F or the leanest cuts of lamb, choose from the leg or sirloin sections.

EXCHANGES

| 1½ STARCH |
| 2 MEDIUM-FAT MEAT |
| 1 FRUIT |

NUTRITION FACTS PER SERVING

		Daily Values
Calories	323	16%
Total fat	11 g	16%
Saturated fat	4 g	21%
Cholesterol	48 mg	15%
Sodium	176 mg	7%
Carbohydrate	41 g	13%
Fiber	1 g	4%
Protein	15 g	

LAMB KABOBS

MAKES 4 SERVINGS   PREP: 20 MINUTES   MARINATE: 4 TO 24 HOURS   BROIL: 10 MINUTES

12 ounces lean boneless lamb
¼ cup snipped fresh parsley
3 tablespoons lemon juice
3 tablespoons water
1 tablespoon olive oil or cooking
     oil
½ teaspoon dried marjoram,
     crushed
½ teaspoon dried thyme, crushed
1 clove garlic, minced
¼ teaspoon black pepper
1 medium red or green sweet
     pepper, cut into 1-inch pieces
4 green onions, cut into 2-inch
     pieces

1. Trim fat from lamb. Cut lamb into 1-inch pieces. Place lamb in a plastic bag set in a deep bowl. For marinade, in a small mixing bowl stir together the parsley, lemon juice, water, oil, marjoram, thyme, garlic, and black pepper. Pour over lamb in bag. Close bag and turn to coat lamb well. Marinate in the refrigerator for 4 to 24 hours, turning the bag occasionally.

2. Cook sweet pepper and green onion pieces in *boiling water* for 1 minute. Drain well. Remove lamb from bag, reserving marinade. On 4 long skewers, alternately thread the meat, sweet pepper, and green onion pieces, leaving about ¼ inch between the pieces.

3. Place the skewers on the unheated rack of a broiler pan. Broil 4 inches from the heat about 10 minutes or to desired doneness, turning and brushing once with the reserved marinade. (Or, grill on the rack of an uncovered grill directly over medium coals for 10 to 14 minutes or to desired doneness, turning and brushing once with the reserved marinade.)

S elect a lamb leg sirloin chop or a portion of a leg of lamb to cut into pieces for these marinated kabobs.

EXCHANGES

| 2 LEAN MEAT |
| ½ VEGETABLE |

NUTRITION FACTS PER SERVING

		Daily Values
Calories	134	7%
Total fat	7 g	11%
Saturated fat	2 g	10%
Cholesterol	43 mg	14%
Sodium	36 mg	2%
Carbohydrate	3 g	1%
Fiber	1 g	4%
Protein	14 g	

SALMON WITH FRUIT SALSA

MAKES 4 SERVINGS   PREP: 15 MINUTES   BROIL: 8 MINUTES

14 to 16 ounces fresh or frozen
  salmon or halibut steaks, cut
  1 inch thick
¾ cup chopped fresh strawberries
  or chopped, peeled peaches
  or nectarines
⅓ cup chopped, peeled kiwifruit
  or fresh apricots
1 tablespoon snipped fresh
  cilantro
1 tablespoon orange or apple juice
1 jalapeño pepper, seeded and
  chopped*
1 teaspoon olive oil or cooking oil
⅛ teaspoon lemon-pepper
  seasoning
  Nonstick spray coating
  Fresh cilantro sprigs (optional)

1. Thaw fish, if frozen. Cut into 4 serving-size pieces. For salsa, in a bowl stir together fruits, 1 tablespoon cilantro, the orange or apple juice, and jalapeño pepper. Set aside.

2. Brush both sides of the fish pieces with the 1 teaspoon olive or cooking oil. Sprinkle with lemon-pepper seasoning. Spray the unheated rack of a broiler pan with nonstick coating. Place fish on rack. Broil 4 inches from the heat for 8 to 12 minutes or until fish flakes easily with a fork, turning once. (Or, spray an unheated grill rack with nonstick coating. Grill fish on an uncovered grill directly over medium-hot coals for 8 to 12 minutes or until fish flakes easily with a fork, turning fish once.) If desired, garnish with cilantro sprigs. Serve with salsa.

*Note: Protect your hands when working with hot peppers by wearing plastic or rubber gloves or working with plastic bags on your hands. If your bare hands touch the peppers, wash your hands and nails well with soap and water. Avoid rubbing your mouth, nose, eyes, or ears.

Packed with B vitamins, protein, and vitamin C, this summer salad (pictured on page 56) packs a nutritional punch with 123 calories.

EXCHANGES

| 2 LEAN MEAT |
| ½ FRUIT |

NUTRITION FACTS PER SERVING

		Daily Values
Calories	123	6%
Total fat	5 g	7%
Saturated fat	1 g	4%.
Cholesterol	18 mg	5%
Sodium	95 mg	3%
Carbohydrate	5 g	1%
Fiber	1 g	4%
Protein	15 g	

CITRUS-TARRAGON SALMON STEAKS

MAKES 4 SERVINGS   PREP: 10 MINUTES   MARINATE: 45 MINUTES   GRILL: 6 TO 9 MINUTES

4 fresh or frozen salmon steaks,
  cut ¾ inch thick (about
  1 pound)
1 teaspoon finely shredded orange
  peel
¼ cup orange juice
¼ cup lime juice
1 tablespoon champagne vinegar
  or white wine vinegar
1 teaspoon olive oil
1 tablespoon snipped fresh
  tarragon or ½ teaspoon dried
  tarragon, crushed
¼ teaspoon salt
⅛ teaspoon pepper

1. Thaw fish, if frozen. For the marinade, stir together the orange peel, orange juice, lime juice, vinegar, olive oil, tarragon, salt, and pepper.

2. Place fish in a shallow nonmetal baking dish. Pour marinade over fish. Cover and marinate in the refrigerator for 45 minutes, turning the fish once. Drain fish, reserving the marinade.

3. Grill fish on a greased grill rack directly over medium coals just until fish begins to flake easily with a fork, turning the fish halfway through the grilling time and brushing with reserved marinade. Allow 4 to 6 minutes per ½-inch thickness.

For a healthful side dish, grill a variety of fresh vegetables alongside these fish steaks.

EXCHANGES

| 3 LEAN MEAT |
| ½ FRUIT |

NUTRITION FACTS PER SERVING

		Daily Values
Calories	179	9%
Total fat	8 g	12%
Saturated fat	1 g	5%
Cholesterol	42 mg	14%
Sodium	184 mg	8%
Carbohydrate	4 g	1%
Fiber	0 g	0%
Protein	24 g	

HONEY-GLAZED SALMON

MAKES 6 SERVINGS   PREP: 10 MINUTES   BROIL: 4 MINUTES PER ½-INCH THICKNESS

Salmon is a good source of omega-3 fatty acids, which help in lowering your risk of heart disease. Try to include fish once or twice a week in your meals.

EXCHANGES
3 LEAN MEAT

NUTRITION FACTS PER SERVING

		Daily Values
Calories	140	7%
Total fat	4 g	6%
Saturated fat	1 g	4%
Cholesterol	20 mg	6%
Sodium	255 mg	10%
Carbohydrate	9 g	2%
Fiber	0 g	0%
Protein	17 g	

1½ **pounds fresh or frozen salmon fillets**
3 **tablespoons honey**
2 **tablespoons sodium-reduced soy sauce**
¼ **teaspoon crushed red pepper**
   Nonstick spray coating

1. Thaw salmon, if frozen. In a small mixing bowl stir together the honey, soy sauce, and red pepper.

2. Measure thickness of fish. Spray the unheated rack of a broiler pan with nonstick coating. Place fish, skin side up, on rack, turning under any thin portions. Broil 4 inches from the heat for 4 minutes per ½-inch thickness. Brush salmon with the honey mixture. If salmon is 1 inch or more thick, turn salmon fillet. Continue to broil until the fish flakes easily with a fork. (Or, to grill, brush fillets with the honey mixture. Place fillets in a well-greased grill basket. Place basket on the rack of an uncovered grill directly over medium-hot coals. Grill just until the fish begins to flake easily with a fork, turning fish halfway through the grilling time. Allow 4 to 6 minutes per ½-inch thickness.)

All Sorts of Salmon

Your market may offer up to several kinds of salmon. Often, you can use different kinds interchangeably, but sometimes your recipe, your budget, or the occasion may require a certain kind.

Shopping for Salmon
Salmon in supermarkets today tend to be uniform in size, color, and flavor because many are raised on fish farms. Some of the ocean-caught salmon still come from off U.S. shores, but a growing number are imported from other countries.

At the fish counter, you'll see salmon meat that ranges in color from the deep orange of sockeye to the light blush of pink. Its flavor can vary from mild to rich, with farm-raised fish having a milder taste than ocean-caught salmon.

Salmon also vary in price. Chinook tends to be most expensive, making it a food for splurging on. Pink usually costs the least. You can buy salmon whole, in fillets and steaks, and canned.

Types of Salmon
Atlantic: This variety of salmon is primarily farmed. The flesh ranges from pink to red or orange. It's somewhat higher in oil than other types of salmon, making it good for grilling or broiling.
Chinook or King: The largest and most expensive salmon from the Pacific Ocean, chinook has soft flesh that ranges from deep pinkish orange to almost white. The oil-rich flesh broils and grills well.
Chum, Keta, or Silverbright: This salmon can range in color from red to light pink. Chum has a slightly coarser texture and less fat than other salmon, so it's best steamed or poached.
Coho or Silver: Often called silver salmon because of its silver-skinned belly and sides, coho's flesh ranges from pink to orange-red in color. Because farm-raised cohos can be smaller than their ocean-swimming cousins, they are a good choice for individual servings of drawn or dressed fish.

Pacific: This term can refer to any of the five salmon species found in the Pacific Ocean: chinook, chum, coho, pink, and sockeye. If you see salmon labeled as Pacific, find out what kind it really is so you'll know how to best prepare it.
Pink: As its name suggests, the flesh of this salmon is light pink. It's the smallest and most abundant variety, and also the least expensive. Its peak season is short, but canning makes it available year-round. Serve pink salmon in casseroles, soups, and sandwiches.
Sockeye, Blueback, or Red: Although it's primarily sold canned, this salmon can be found fresh during the summer months. The deep red color, firm flesh, and moderate fat content make sockeye salmon a good choice for baking. Serve it warm or chilled. Break it into chunks for salads, pastas, and appetizer toppings.

CREAMY FISH CHOWDER

MAKES 4 SERVINGS   PREP: 10 MINUTES   COOK: 20 MINUTES

8 ounces fresh or frozen skinless sole, flounder, or orange roughy fillets (about ½ inch thick)
2 cups loose-pack frozen broccoli, cauliflower, and carrots
1 14½-ounce can reduced-sodium chicken broth
½ cup chopped onion
½ cup chopped red sweet pepper
1 teaspoon finely shredded lemon peel
1 teaspoon dried dillweed
⅛ teaspoon black pepper
  Dash salt
1 12-ounce can evaporated skim milk
3 tablespoons all-purpose flour

1. Thaw fish, if frozen. Cut fish into ¾-inch pieces. Cover and refrigerate fish until needed.

2. In a large saucepan stir together frozen vegetables, chicken broth, onion, sweet pepper, lemon peel, dillweed, black pepper, and salt. Bring to boiling; reduce heat. Simmer, covered, for 5 minutes.

3. In a screw-top jar combine the evaporated skim milk and flour; cover and shake until smooth. Stir into mixture in saucepan. Cook and stir until thickened and bubbly. Cook and stir for 1 minute more. Stir in fish. Cover and gently simmer about 3 minutes or until fish flakes easily with a fork.

Rich-tasting fish chowder can still be on the menu when you make it with low-fat evaporated skim milk.

EXCHANGES

| 1½ LEAN MEAT |
| 2 VEGETABLE |
| ½ MILK |

NUTRITION FACTS PER SERVING

		Daily Values
Calories	171	8%
Total fat	1 g	2%
Saturated fat	0 g	1%
Cholesterol	29 mg	9%
Sodium	484 mg	20%
Carbohydrate	20 g	6%
Fiber	2 g	8%
Protein	19 g	

QUICK CREOLE

MAKES 4 SERVINGS   PREP: 20 MINUTES

1 pound fresh or frozen catfish fillets or medium shelled shrimp, or 2 cups cubed cooked chicken
2 14½-ounce cans Cajun-style stewed tomatoes
½ cup chopped green sweet pepper
2 tablespoons all-purpose flour
2 teaspoons white wine Worcestershire sauce or Worcestershire sauce
  Few dashes bottled hot pepper sauce (optional)
1 bay leaf
2 cups hot cooked rice

1. Thaw catfish or shrimp, if frozen. If using catfish, cut into 1-inch pieces and remove skin. If using shrimp, devein. Cut up large pieces of stewed tomatoes. Set aside.

2. In a medium saucepan combine *undrained* tomatoes, sweet pepper, flour, Worcestershire sauce, hot pepper sauce (if desired), and bay leaf. Cook and stir until thickened and bubbly.

3. Add fish, shrimp, or cooked chicken; cover and simmer for 3 to 5 minutes more or until done. (When done, the catfish should flake easily with a fork, and shrimp should turn pink. Chicken should be heated through.) Discard bay leaf. Serve over hot cooked rice.

Microwave Directions: In a 2-quart microwave-safe casserole combine the *undrained* tomatoes, sweet pepper, flour, Worcestershire sauce, hot pepper sauce (if desired), and bay leaf. Cook, uncovered, on 100% power (high) for 5 to 8 minutes or until bubbly, stirring after every minute until slightly thickened, then stirring every 30 seconds. Add fish, shrimp, or cooked chicken; cover. Cook on high for 3 to 5 minutes or until done, stirring once. Discard bay leaf.

Cajun-style stewed tomatoes add spunk to this dish. If you're watching sodium, use low-sodium stewed tomatoes and ground red pepper (¼ teaspoon).

EXCHANGES

| 1½ STARCH |
| 2½ VERY LEAN MEAT |
| 2 VEGETABLE |

NUTRITION FACTS PER SERVING

		Daily Values
Calories	270	13%
Total fat	3 g	5%
Saturated fat	1 g	5%
Cholesterol	61 mg	20%
Sodium	782 mg	32%
Carbohydrate	40 g	13%
Fiber	0 g	0%
Protein	20 g	

ZUPPA DI PESCE
MAKES 4 SERVINGS   PREP: 30 MINUTES

The Italian name translates as fish soup. It is traditionally served over Crostini or toast. (Soup pictured on page 61.)

EXCHANGES
2 VERY LEAN MEAT
2 VEGETABLE
½ FAT

NUTRITION FACTS PER SERVING
		Daily Values
Calories	165	8%
Total fat	4 g	5%
Saturated fat	1 g	2%
Cholesterol	87 mg	28%
Sodium	459 mg	19%
Carbohydrate	12 g	4%
Fiber	2 g	9%
Protein	19 g	

8 ounces fresh or frozen skinless cod or sea bass fillets
6 ounces fresh or frozen peeled, deveined shrimp
⅓ cup chopped onion
2 stalks celery, sliced
1 clove garlic, minced
2 teaspoons olive oil
1 cup reduced-sodium chicken broth
¼ cup dry white wine or reduced-sodium chicken broth
1 14½-ounce can low-sodium tomatoes, cut up
1 8-ounce can low-sodium tomato sauce
1 teaspoon dried oregano, crushed
¼ teaspoon salt
⅛ teaspoon coarsely ground pepper
1 tablespoon snipped fresh parsley
Fresh oregano sprigs (optional)
1 recipe Crostini (optional)

1. Thaw fish and shrimp, if frozen. Cut fish into 1½-inch pieces. Cut shrimp in half. Cover and refrigerate shrimp and fish until needed.

2. For soup, in a large saucepan cook onion, celery, and garlic in olive oil until tender. Carefully stir in broth and wine or additional broth. Bring to boiling; reduce heat. Simmer, uncovered, for 5 minutes. Stir in drained tomatoes, tomato sauce, oregano, salt, and pepper. Return to boiling; reduce heat. Simmer, covered, for 5 minutes.

3. Gently stir in fish and shrimp. Return just to boiling; reduce heat to low. Simmer, covered, for 3 to 5 minutes or until fish flakes easily with a fork and shrimp turn pink. Stir in parsley. Ladle into serving bowls. If desired, garnish with oregano sprigs and top with Crostini.

Crostini: Lightly spray both sides of six ½-inch-thick slices of Italian bread with *nonstick olive oil spray coating*. Sprinkle with ½ teaspoon *dried thyme* or *rosemary*, crushed. Place on a baking sheet. Bake in a 350° oven for 10 to 15 minutes or until golden brown, turning once.

CRISPY BAKED HALIBUT
MAKES 4 SERVINGS   PREP: 15 MINUTES   COOK: 8 TO 15 MINUTES

When you have a craving for "fried" chicken, you can use this recipe with boneless chicken breasts.

EXCHANGES
4 VERY LEAN MEAT
½ FAT

NUTRITION FACTS PER SERVING
		Daily Values
Calories	174	9%
Total fat	6 g	9%
Saturated fat	1 g	5%
Cholesterol	39 mg	13%
Sodium	158 mg	7%
Carbohydrate	4 g	1%
Fiber	0 g	0%
Protein	26 g	

1¼ pounds fresh or frozen halibut steaks, cut 1 inch thick, or 4 skinless, boneless chicken breast halves (about 1 pound total)
2 teaspoons cooking oil
¾ cup soft sourdough bread crumbs or other bread crumbs
2 tablespoons grated Parmesan cheese
1 tablespoon snipped fresh tarragon or ½ teaspoon dried tarragon, crushed
½ teaspoon paprika
Dash pepper

1. Thaw the fish or chicken, if frozen. Cut fish into 4 portions; pat dry with paper towels and brush with cooking oil. In a shallow dish combine bread crumbs, Parmesan cheese, tarragon, paprika, and pepper. Dip fish or chicken into crumb mixture to coat both sides. Arrange pieces in a 2-quart rectangular baking dish. Sprinkle any leftover bread crumb mixture on top.

2. Bake the fish, uncovered, in a 450° oven for 8 to 12 minutes or until the fish flakes easily with a fork. Do not turn during baking. (Or, bake the chicken, uncovered, about 15 minutes or until chicken is tender and no longer pink.)

TUNA-PASTA SALAD

MAKES 4 SERVINGS   PREP: 25 MINUTES   CHILL: 2 HOURS

3 ounces packaged dried corkscrew macaroni (about 1 cup)
1 medium carrot, thinly sliced
½ of a medium cucumber, quartered lengthwise and sliced
½ of a red sweet pepper, chopped
2 green onions, sliced
⅓ cup reduced-calorie creamy Italian or ranch salad dressing
1 6-ounce can low-sodium chunk light tuna, drained
Romaine or lettuce leaves or thinly sliced tomato

1. Cook pasta according to package directions, except omit any oil and salt. Drain. Rinse with *cold water*; drain.

2. In a large mixing bowl toss together drained pasta, carrot, cucumber, sweet pepper, and onions. Add salad dressing. Toss until well mixed. Gently stir in tuna. Cover and refrigerate for 2 to 6 hours.

3. Arrange greens or tomato on 4 plates. Place a scoop of tuna mixture on greens or tomato on each plate.

Read the nutrition label when selecting salad dressing. Reduced-calorie dressings vary greatly in the number of calories per serving. (Salad pictured on page 62.)

EXCHANGES
1 STARCH
1 LEAN MEAT
1 VEGETABLE

NUTRITION FACTS PER SERVING

		Daily Values
Calories	166	8%
Total fat	3 g	5%
Saturated fat	0 g	0%
Cholesterol	1 mg	0%
Sodium	261 mg	11%
Carbohydrate	22 g	7%
Fiber	2 g	8%
Protein	13 g	

SALMON HASH WITH POTATOES AND PEPPERS

MAKES 4 SERVINGS   PREP: 35 MINUTES

1 pound potatoes (3 medium)
1 cup water
1 medium red sweet pepper, chopped
1 medium green sweet pepper, chopped
½ cup reduced-sodium chicken broth
½ cup chopped onion
1 teaspoon dried basil, crushed
¼ teaspoon dried thyme, crushed
⅛ teaspoon salt
⅛ teaspoon pepper
1 7½-ounce can low-sodium salmon, drained, flaked, and skin and bones removed
½ cup drained, canned whole-kernel corn
Snipped fresh parsley (optional)

1. If desired, peel potatoes. Dice potatoes. In a large skillet bring the water to boiling. Add potatoes; cover and cook for 20 to 25 minutes or until tender. Drain; return potatoes to skillet.

2. Stir the sweet peppers, chicken broth, onion, basil, thyme, salt, and pepper into the potatoes in the skillet. Cover and simmer for 5 minutes or until sweet peppers are tender. Stir in salmon and corn. Cover and cook 2 to 3 minutes more or until heated through. If desired, garnish with snipped parsley.

This easy one-dish dinner brings color, flavor, and a change of pace to the table.

EXCHANGES
2 STARCH
1½ LEAN MEAT
½ VEGETABLE

NUTRITION FACTS PER SERVING

		Daily Values
Calories	228	11%
Total fat	3 g	5%
Saturated fat	0 g	0%
Cholesterol	0 mg	0%
Sodium	204 mg	9%
Carbohydrate	34 g	11%
Fiber	2 g	8%
Protein	15 g	

Tuna-Pasta Salad

VEGETABLE LASAGNA

MAKES 10 SERVINGS   PREP: 30 MINUTES   BAKE: 35 MINUTES   STAND: 10 MINUTES

This meatless lasagna supplies 20 percent of the calcium, 25 percent of the vitamin A, and more than 50 percent of the vitamin C you need in a day.

EXCHANGES

| 1 STARCH |
| 2 VERY LEAN MEAT |
| 1 VEGETABLE |
| ½ FAT |

NUTRITION FACTS PER SERVING

		Daily Values
Calories	195	9%
Total fat	4 g	6%
Saturated fat	1 g	7%
Cholesterol	15 mg	5%
Sodium	299 mg	12%
Carbohydrate	24 g	8%
Fiber	2 g	8%
Protein	18 g	

9 lasagna noodles
1 15-ounce carton fat-free ricotta cheese
⅔ cup refrigerated or frozen egg product, thawed
2 tablespoons snipped fresh basil or 1 teaspoon dried basil, crushed
¼ teaspoon black pepper
   Nonstick spray coating
½ cup chopped onion
½ cup chopped red or green sweet pepper
1 clove garlic, minced
1 cup reduced-sodium chicken broth
1 cup skim milk
¼ cup all-purpose flour
¼ teaspoon salt
1 cup shredded reduced-fat mozzarella cheese (4 ounces)
2 10-ounce packages frozen chopped broccoli, thawed and well drained
   Nonstick spray coating
¼ cup finely shredded Parmesan cheese
1 medium tomato, seeded and chopped

1. Cook lasagna noodles according to package directions, except omit any oil and salt. Drain. Rinse with *cold water*; drain. Set aside.

2. In a medium mixing bowl stir together the ricotta cheese, egg product, basil, and black pepper. Set aside.

3. Spray an unheated medium saucepan with nonstick coating. Preheat over medium heat. Add onion, sweet pepper, and garlic; cook and stir until onion is tender. Stir chicken broth into vegetables in saucepan.

4. In a screw-top jar combine milk, flour, and salt. Cover and shake until combined. Stir into mixture in saucepan. Cook and stir until thickened and bubbly. Cook and stir for 1 minute more. Remove from heat. Stir in mozzarella cheese until melted. Stir in broccoli.

5. Spray a 3-quart rectangular baking dish with nonstick coating. Arrange 3 cooked lasagna noodles in the bottom of the dish. Top with one-third of the ricotta mixture and one-third of the broccoli mixture. Repeat layers 2 more times, using the remaining noodles, ricotta mixture, and broccoli mixture. Sprinkle with Parmesan cheese. Bake in a 375° oven for 35 to 40 minutes or until heated through. Let stand for 10 minutes. Sprinkle with the chopped tomato. To serve, cut into squares.

Herb Basics

Whether you're watching fat, calories, sodium, or all three, good flavor remains the most important element in any dish. Fresh and dried herbs are an easy way to boost the way ingredients taste in many dishes.

Fresh herbs are available in most supermarkets year-round. Use kitchen shears to quickly snip the amount you need. If you are substituting a fresh herb for dried, use about three times more fresh than dried herb (1½ teaspoons fresh snipped herb instead of ½ teaspoon dried herb). A fresh herb sprig makes an easy garnish and brings new life to the most ordinary dish.

Store dried herbs in tightly covered containers in a dark place to protect them from air and light. Do not freeze dried herbs or store them near hot appliances.

Replace dried herbs about once a year or whenever you notice their aroma has become weak.

To use a dried herb, measure it, place it in the palm of one hand, and crush it with your other hand to release its flavor.

When cooking herbs, add dried herbs at the beginning of cooking to draw out their flavors; add fresh herbs at the end of cooking to retain their flavors.

BEAN AND CORN TAMALE PIE

MAKES 6 SERVINGS   PREP: 25 MINUTES   BAKE: 20 MINUTES

⅓ cup water
¾ cup chopped onion
½ cup sliced carrot
2 15- to 16-ounce cans beans, rinsed and drained (any combination of kidney beans, black beans, great northern beans, navy beans, garbanzo beans, small white beans, pinto beans, or small red beans)
1 cup frozen whole kernel corn
1 15-ounce can low-sodium tomato sauce
1 4½-ounce can diced green chili peppers, drained
1 clove garlic, minced
1½ teaspoons chili powder
½ teaspoon ground cumin
¼ teaspoon black pepper
1 8½-ounce package corn muffin mix
2 slightly beaten egg whites
⅓ cup skim milk

1. In a large saucepan bring the water to boiling. Add the onion and carrot. Return to boiling; reduce heat. Simmer, covered, about 5 minutes or until tender. Do not drain. Stir in beans, corn, tomato sauce, *half* of the chili peppers, the garlic, chili powder, cumin, and black pepper. Cook and stir until heated through. Cover; keep warm while preparing topping.

2. For topping, in a small mixing bowl stir together the muffin mix, egg whites, milk, and remaining chili peppers just until mixed.

3. Spoon hot bean mixture into a 2-quart rectangular baking dish. Spoon topping evenly over bean mixture. Bake in a 400° oven about 20 minutes or until a wooden toothpick inserted in center of topping comes out clean.

Who'd believe tamale pie could be part of a healthful diet? This meatless version has only 6 grams fat per serving.

EXCHANGES

| 3 STARCH |
| 1 VERY LEAN MEAT |
| 3 VEGETABLE |

NUTRITION FACTS PER SERVING

		Daily Values
Calories	347	17%
Total fat	6 g	9%
Saturated fat	1 g	5%
Cholesterol	0 mg	0%
Sodium	670 mg	27%
Carbohydrate	65 g	21%
Fiber	10 g	40%
Protein	16 g	

CHILI-SAUCED PASTA

MAKES 3 SERVINGS   PREP: 15 MINUTES

6 ounces refrigerated linguine
1 14½-ounce can reduced-sodium stewed tomatoes
1 medium green sweet pepper, cut into 2-inch-long thin strips
2 tablespoons reduced-sodium tomato paste
1 tablespoon chili powder
¼ teaspoon salt
¼ teaspoon garlic powder
¼ teaspoon ground cumin
1 8-ounce can kidney beans, rinsed and drained
¼ cup cold water
2 teaspoons cornstarch

1. Cook pasta according to package directions, except omit any salt. Drain. Set aside and keep warm.

2. Meanwhile, in a medium saucepan combine tomatoes, sweet pepper strips, tomato paste, chili powder, salt, garlic powder, and cumin. Bring to boiling; reduce heat. Simmer, covered, for 3 minutes. Stir in kidney beans.

3. Stir together cold water and cornstarch; add to tomato mixture. Cook and stir until thickened and bubbly. Cook and stir for 2 minutes more. Serve tomato mixture over hot pasta.

You can use dried pasta instead of fresh in this 15-minute recipe, but plan on adding from 6 to 8 more minutes to the cooking time.

EXCHANGES

| 3 STARCH |
| 1 VERY LEAN MEAT |
| 2 VEGETABLE |

NUTRITION FACTS PER SERVING

		Daily Values
Calories	322	16%
Total fat	2 g	3%
Saturated fat	0g	0%
Cholesterol	49 mg	16%
Sodium	392 mg	16%
Carbohydrate	65 g	22%
Fiber	10 g	40%
Protein	15 g	

CURRIED LENTILS AND VEGETABLES

MAKES 6 SERVINGS   PREP: 20 MINUTES   COOK: 30 MINUTES

Compared to dried beans, lentils take a shorter time to cook—just 25 to 30 minutes.

EXCHANGES

| 2 STARCH |
| 1 VERY LEAN MEAT |
| 1 VEGETABLE |
| ½ MILK |

NUTRITION FACTS PER SERVING

		Daily Values
Calories	262	13%
Total fat	1 g	1%
Saturated fat	0 g	0%
Cholesterol	1 mg	0%
Sodium	363 mg	15%
Carbohydrate	46 g	15%
Fiber	4 g	17%
Protein	19 g	

2 cups dry lentils (12 ounces)
4 cups water
1½ cups chopped carrot
1½ cups chopped onion
1 cup chopped celery
1 clove garlic, minced
1 tablespoon curry powder
1 teaspoon grated gingerroot
¾ teaspoon salt
1 medium tomato, chopped
1 tablespoon snipped fresh parsley or cilantro (optional)
1½ cups plain fat-free yogurt or fat-free dairy sour cream

1. Rinse lentils. Drain.

2. In a large saucepan combine the water, lentils, carrot, onion, celery, garlic, curry powder, gingerroot, and salt. Bring to boiling; reduce heat. Simmer, covered, for 25 to 30 minutes or until lentils are tender.

3. To serve, top the lentil mixture with tomato. If desired, sprinkle with snipped parsley or cilantro. Top with yogurt or sour cream.

VEGETABLE-MACARONI CASSEROLE

MAKES 4 SERVINGS   PREP: 15 MINUTES   BAKE: 15 MINUTES   STAND: 5 MINUTES

Need to find a way to get your kids to eat vegetables? Try this perennial favorite packed with vegetables.

EXCHANGES

| 2 STARCH |
| 2 VEGETABLE |
| ½ MILK |

NUTRITION FACTS PER SERVING

		Daily Values
Calories	261	13%
Total fat	2 g	3%
Saturated fat	1 g	5%
Cholesterol	8 mg	3%
Sodium	404 mg	17%
Carbohydrate	45 g	15%
Fiber	1 g	5%
Protein	15 g	

¾ cup packaged dried elbow macaroni
1 10-ounce package frozen mixed vegetables
1 medium zucchini, halved lengthwise and sliced
1 12-ounce can evaporated skim milk
½ cup reduced-sodium chicken broth
¼ cup all-purpose flour
½ teaspoon dried oregano, crushed
¼ teaspoon garlic salt
⅛ teaspoon pepper
Nonstick spray coating
1 medium tomato, sliced
3 tablespoons grated Parmesan cheese

1. In a large saucepan cook macaroni according to package directions, except omit any oil and salt. Add mixed vegetables and zucchini for the last 3 minutes of cooking. Drain. Return pasta mixture to the saucepan.

2. Meanwhile, in a medium saucepan whisk together evaporated skim milk, chicken broth, flour, oregano, garlic salt, and pepper. Cook and stir until thickened and bubbly. Add to pasta mixture; toss to coat. Spray a 2-quart square baking dish with nonstick coating. Spoon macaroni mixture into dish.

3. Bake in a 375° oven for 10 minutes. Top with sliced tomato and sprinkle with grated Parmesan cheese. Bake about 5 minutes more or until heated through. Let stand for 5 minutes before serving.

SPINACH- AND RICOTTA-STUFFED TOMATOES

MAKES 4 SERVINGS   PREP: 25 MINUTES   BAKE: 20 MINUTES

4 large tomatoes
6 ounces fresh spinach (6 cups)
½ cup finely chopped onion
2 cloves garlic, minced
1 tablespoon olive oil
⅔ cup fat-free ricotta cheese
1½ teaspoons snipped fresh basil or
    ½ teaspoon dried basil,
    crushed
¼ teaspoon pepper
⅛ teaspoon salt
2 tablespoons fine dry bread
    crumbs
1 tablespoon grated Parmesan
    cheese

1. Cut a thin slice off the stem end of each tomato. Hollow out the tomatoes, leaving a ¼- to ½-inch-thick shell. Discard seeds. Chop the tomato insides. Set aside.

2. Wash spinach. Place wet spinach in a large skillet. Cover and cook over medium-high heat for 2 to 3 minutes or just until spinach wilts. Drain well. Chop spinach. Set aside.

3. Wipe skillet out with paper towels. In the same skillet cook onion and garlic in olive oil until tender. Remove from heat. Stir in chopped tomato, spinach, ricotta cheese, basil, pepper, and salt. Spoon into the tomato shells. Place in a shallow baking dish.

4. Stir together bread crumbs and Parmesan cheese. Sprinkle the mixture over tomatoes. Bake in a 350° oven for 20 minutes or until heated through and the tops are golden brown.

This meatless entrée is a good source of vitamin A and vitamin C, and it provides protein.

EXCHANGES

| 1 VERY LEAN MEAT |
| 2 VEGETABLE |
| 1 FAT |

NUTRITION FACTS PER SERVING

		Daily Values
Calories	119	5%
Total fat	5 g	6%
Saturated fat	1 g	4%
Cholesterol	5 mg	1%
Sodium	174 mg	7%
Carbohydrate	14 g	4%
Fiber	3 g	12%
Protein	9 g	

PINTO BEAN AND CHEESE BURRITOS

MAKES 8 SERVINGS   PREP: 12 MINUTES   BAKE: 15 MINUTES

8 8-inch whole wheat or flour
    tortillas
2 15-ounce cans pinto beans,
    rinsed and drained
    Nonstick spray coating
½ cup sliced green onions
1 cup shredded reduced-fat
    Monterey Jack or cheddar
    cheese (4 ounces)
½ cup salsa
¼ cup light dairy sour cream
    Snipped fresh cilantro or
    parsley (optional)

1. Wrap tortillas in foil. Heat in a 350° oven for 15 minutes or until heated through. Meanwhile, mash beans slightly with the back of a spoon.

2. Spray a baking sheet with nonstick coating. On each tortilla, place some of the beans, green onions, and cheese. Fold in 2 sides of each tortilla, then roll up. Arrange burritos, seam sides down, on prepared baking sheet. Bake in the 350° oven for 15 minutes or until heated through. Serve burritos topped with salsa and sour cream. If desired, sprinkle with snipped cilantro or parsley.

You don't need to run out for take-out burritos (which usually are high in fat). Make these at home and *know* they're good for you.

EXCHANGES

| 2 STARCH |
| 1 MEDIUM-FAT MEAT |
| ½ VEGETABLE |

NUTRITION FACTS PER BURRITO

		Daily Values
Calories	263	13%
Total fat	6 g	9%
Saturated fat	2 g	10%
Cholesterol	11 mg	4%
Sodium	677 mg	28%
Carbohydrate	39 g	13%
Fiber	5 g	25%
Protein	14 g	

SPINACH SOUFFLÉ IN CORNMEAL CREPES

MAKES 6 SERVINGS   PREP: 45 MINUTES   BAKE: 15 MINUTES

Parmesan-flavored spinach soufflé fills these savory cornmeal crepes. They're just right for a light meal or try them for brunch served with fresh fruit (pictured on page 69).

EXCHANGES

1 STARCH
½ LEAN MEAT
1 VEGETABLE

NUTRITION FACTS PER SERVING

		Daily Values
Calories	131	6%
Total fat	4 g	6%
Saturated fat	1 g	5%
Cholesterol	38 mg	12%
Sodium	182 mg	7%
Carbohydrate	16 g	5%
Fiber	1 g	3%
Protein	9 g	

1 recipe Cornmeal Crepes
  Nonstick spray coating
½ cup chopped onion
1 clove garlic, minced
⅔ cup skim milk
2 tablespoons all-purpose flour
⅛ teaspoon salt
⅛ teaspoon pepper
⅛ teaspoon ground nutmeg
1 beaten egg yolk
½ of a 10-ounce package frozen chopped spinach, thawed and well drained
2 tablespoons grated Parmesan cheese
3 egg whites
⅛ teaspoon cream of tartar
1 cup cherry tomatoes, coarsely chopped
  Fresh basil sprigs

1. Prepare Cornmeal Crepes. Set aside. Spray a 3-quart rectangular baking dish with nonstick coating. Set aside.

2. Spray an unheated medium saucepan with nonstick coating. Preheat over medium heat. Add onion and garlic. Cook and stir until onion is tender. In a screw-top jar combine milk, flour, salt, pepper, and nutmeg. Cover and shake to combine. Add to vegetables in saucepan. Cook and stir until thickened and bubbly. Gradually stir about half of the hot mixture into the beaten egg yolk. Return all to saucepan. Stir in spinach and Parmesan cheese. Heat through.

3. In a small mixing bowl beat the egg whites and cream of tartar with an electric mixer on medium to high speed until stiff peaks form (tips stand straight). Stir about one-fourth of the beaten egg whites into the spinach mixture to lighten. Fold remaining beaten egg whites into the spinach mixture.

4. Spoon ¼ cup spinach mixture on unbrowned side of each crepe, spreading evenly. Fold crepe in half then in half again, forming wedges. Place filled crepes in prepared baking dish. Bake, uncovered, in a 375° oven for 15 to 20 minutes or until heated through. To serve, place 2 filled crepes on each serving plate. Sprinkle with chopped tomato and garnish with basil.

Cornmeal Crepes: In a small mixing bowl combine 1 cup *skim milk;* ⅓ cup *all-purpose flour;* ¼ cup *refrigerated* or *frozen egg product,* thawed; 2 tablespoons *cornmeal;* and 2 teaspoons *cooking oil.* Beat with a rotary beater until well mixed. Spray an unheated 6-inch nonstick skillet with *nonstick spray coating.* Heat over medium heat. Remove from heat. Spoon about 2 tablespoons of the batter into the skillet. Lift and tilt skillet to spread batter. Return to heat. Brown on 1 side only (30 to 60 seconds). (Or, cook on an inverted crepe maker according to the manufacturer's directions.) Stir batter occasionally. Repeat with remaining batter, making 12 crepes total. If necessary, lightly brush the skillet with cooking oil to prevent crepes from sticking.*

*****Note:** Spraying a hot skillet with nonstick coating is not recommended.

SIDE DISHES

■ STARCH/BREAD   ■ MEAT   ■ VEGETABLE   ■ FRUIT   ■ MILK   ■ FAT

On left: *Chilled Asparagus Salad, page 72*

CHILLED ASPARAGUS SALAD

MAKES 6 SERVINGS   PREP: 20 MINUTES   CHILL: AT LEAST 30 MINUTES

Wash asparagus well to remove all grit from the tips before cooking. (Salad pictured on page 70.)

½ cup fat-free mayonnaise dressing or salad dressing
¼ cup plain fat-free yogurt
½ teaspoon finely shredded orange peel
⅓ cup orange juice
⅛ teaspoon lemon-pepper seasoning
1½ pounds fresh asparagus spears or two 10-ounce packages frozen asparagus spears
Orange peel strips (optional)

1. For dressing, in a small bowl stir together mayonnaise dressing or salad dressing, yogurt, orange peel, orange juice, and lemon-pepper seasoning. Cover and refrigerate until serving time.

2. If using fresh asparagus, snap off and discard woody bases. If desired, scrape off scales. Cook in a covered saucepan, in a small amount of *boiling water* about 4 to 6 minutes or until crisp-tender. If using frozen asparagus, cook according to package directions.

3. Drain asparagus. Immediately plunge cooked asparagus into *ice water*. When chilled, drain. Cover and refrigerate until serving time.

4. Just before serving, arrange chilled asparagus spears on serving plates. Drizzle dressing over asparagus. If desired, garnish with orange peel strips.

EXCHANGES
2 VEGETABLE

NUTRITION FACTS PER SERVING

		Daily Values
Calories	47	2%
Total fat	0 g	0%
Saturated fat	0 g	0%
Cholesterol	0 mg	0%
Sodium	287 mg	11%
Carbohydrate	10 g	3%
Fiber	2 g	6%
Protein	3 g	

VEGETABLE CHOWDER

MAKES 6 SERVINGS   PREP: 20 MINUTES   COOK: 5 MINUTES

This chowder gets its richness from the evaporated skim milk. The milk also can be used in place of cream in soups or casseroles.

1 14½-ounce can reduced-sodium chicken broth
1 cup frozen cut broccoli or cut green beans
1 cup frozen whole kernel corn
1 cup sliced fresh mushrooms
½ cup sliced green onions
¼ cup finely chopped red sweet pepper
1 12-ounce can evaporated skim milk
2 tablespoons all-purpose flour
1 teaspoon snipped fresh dillweed or ¼ teaspoon dried dillweed
⅛ teaspoon garlic salt
⅛ teaspoon black pepper

1. In a medium saucepan combine broth, broccoli or beans, corn, mushrooms, green onions, and sweet pepper. Bring to boiling; reduce heat. Cover and simmer for 5 minutes.

2. Meanwhile, in a screw-top jar combine evaporated skim milk, flour, dillweed, garlic salt, and black pepper. Cover and shake to combine. Gradually stir into mixture in saucepan. Cook and stir until thickened and bubbly. Cook and stir for 1 minute more.

EXCHANGES
½ STARCH
½ VEGETABLE
½ MILK

NUTRITION FACTS PER SERVING

		Daily Values
Calories	92	4%
Total fat	1 g	1%
Saturated fat	0 g	0%
Cholesterol	2 mg	0%
Sodium	308 mg	12%
Carbohydrate	16 g	5%
Fiber	1 g	4%
Protein	7 g	

VEGETABLE PASTA SALAD

MAKES 6 SERVINGS   PREP: 25 MINUTES   CHILL: 2 TO 24 HOURS

4 ounces packaged dried
 corkscrew macaroni
 (about 1⅓ cups)
½ of a 0.7- to 1.6-ounce envelope
 Italian dry salad dressing mix
3 tablespoons water
2 tablespoons frozen orange juice
 concentrate, thawed
2 tablespoons salad oil
2 cups small broccoli flowerets or
 sliced, halved zucchini
1 cup chopped, seeded tomato
2 tablespoons sliced green onion
¼ cup sliced radishes

1. Cook macaroni according to package directions, except omit any oil or salt. Drain. Rinse with *cold water;* drain.

2. For dressing, in a screw-top jar combine the dry salad dressing mix, water, orange juice concentrate, and oil. Cover and shake until well combined.

3. In a large mixing bowl toss together macaroni, broccoli or zucchini, tomato, and green onion. Add dressing. Toss to coat. Cover and refrigerate for 2 to 24 hours.

4. To serve, stir sliced radishes into macaroni mixture.

Packaged Italian salad dressing mix gets a flavor boost by using orange juice concentrate instead of just water.

EXCHANGES

| 1 STARCH |
| 1 VEGETABLE |
| 1 FAT |

NUTRITION FACTS PER SERVING

		Daily Values
Calories	148	7%
Total fat	5 g	8%
Saturated fat	1 g	3%
Cholesterol	0 mg	0%
Sodium	240 g	9%
Carbohydrate	22 g	7%
Fiber	2 g	9%
Protein	4 g	

VEGETABLES WITH FETA CHEESE SAUCE

MAKES 4 SERVINGS   PREP: 15 MINUTES   COOK: 6 MINUTES

2 cups broccoli flowerets
2 cups cauliflower flowerets
½ cup chopped red sweet pepper
½ cup reduced-sodium
 chicken broth
½ cup skim milk
1 tablespoon all-purpose flour
¼ teaspoon black pepper
⅛ teaspoon garlic powder
½ cup crumbled feta cheese
 (2 ounces)

1. In a medium saucepan combine broccoli, cauliflower, sweet pepper, and chicken broth. Bring to boiling; reduce heat. Simmer, covered, for 6 to 8 minutes or until almost crisp-tender.

2. In a screw-top jar combine milk, flour, black pepper, and garlic powder. Cover and shake until combined. Stir into vegetable mixture in saucepan. Cook and stir until thickened and bubbly. Cook and stir for 1 minute more. Remove from heat. Stir in feta cheese until nearly melted, then serve.

Feta cheese, often used in Greek dishes, has a delicious tang and adds richness to the sauce.

EXCHANGES

| ½ MEDIUM-FAT MEAT |
| 2 VEGETABLE |

NUTRITION FACTS PER SERVING

		Daily Values
Calories	97	4%
Total fat	4 g	5%
Saturated fat	2 g	11%
Cholesterol	13 mg	4%
Sodium	276 mg	11%
Carbohydrate	11 g	3%
Fiber	4 g	16%
Protein	7 g	

MIXED GREENS AND FRUIT SALAD

MAKES 4 SERVINGS   PREP: 15 MINUTES

4 cups torn mixed greens
1 cup sliced fresh mushrooms
1 cup fresh blueberries, raspberries, quartered strawberries, and/or canned mandarin orange sections, drained
1/3 cup orange juice
4 teaspoons salad oil
4 teaspoons brown mustard
1½ teaspoons sugar
1½ teaspoons snipped fresh mint or ¼ teaspoon dried mint, crushed
¼ teaspoon salt
1/8 teaspoon pepper

1. In a large bowl gently toss together greens, mushrooms, and fruit.

2. For dressing, in a screw-top jar combine orange juice, oil, brown mustard, sugar, mint, salt, and pepper. Cover and shake until combined. Drizzle over salad. Toss to coat.

Enjoy this tossed salad (pictured on page 74) with fresh berries in the summer months or with canned mandarin orange sections during winter.

EXCHANGES

| 1 VEGETABLE |
| ½ FRUIT |
| 1 FAT |

NUTRITION FACTS PER SERVING

		Daily Values
Calories	97	4%
Total fat	5 g	8%
Saturated fat	1 g	3%
Cholesterol	0 g	0%
Sodium	248 mg	10%
Carbohydrate	12 g	3%
Fiber	3 g	11%
Protein	3 g	

LEMON MAPLE CARROTS

MAKES 4 SERVINGS   PREP: 5 MINUTES   COOK: 5 MINUTES

3 cups packaged, peeled baby carrots
2 tablespoons maple syrup or maple-flavored syrup
1 teaspoon margarine or butter, melted
½ teaspoon finely shredded lemon peel

1. Place carrots in the top of a steamer over *boiling water*. Steam, covered, for 5 to 8 minutes or until the carrots are crisp-tender.

2. Meanwhile, in a small bowl stir together the syrup, margarine or butter, and lemon peel. Pour syrup mixture over hot carrots. Toss to coat. Serve immediately.

Tart lemon contrasts with the sweet maple syrup on these carrots.

EXCHANGES

| 2 VEGETABLE |
| ½ FRUIT |

NUTRITION FACTS PER SERVING

		Daily Values
Calories	81	4%
Total fat	1 g	1%
Saturated fat	0 g	1%
Cholesterol	0 mg	0%
Sodium	81 mg	3%
Carbohydrate	17 g	5%
Fiber	4 g	14%
Protein	1 g	

Mixed Greens and Fruit Salad

Wax beans are a pale yellow variety of green beans. They're most abundant between May and October.

EXCHANGES

2 VEGETABLE

NUTRITION FACTS PER SERVING

		Daily Values
Calories	51	2%
Total fat	1 g	1%
Saturated fat	0 g	1%
Cholesterol	3 mg	1%
Sodium	92 mg	3%
Carbohydrate	9 g	3%
Fiber	3 g	11%
Protein	3 g	

WAX BEANS WITH TOMATOES
MAKES 4 TO 6 SERVINGS   PREP: 10 MINUTES   COOK: 25 MINUTES

12 ounces fresh wax beans or
    green beans
¼ cup chopped onion
¼ cup finely chopped Canadian-
    style bacon or cooked ham
1 medium tomato, chopped
1½ teaspoons snipped fresh basil or
    ½ teaspoon dried basil,
    crushed
⅛ teaspoon pepper

1. Remove ends and strings from wax or green beans. Cut beans into bite-size pieces.

2. In a covered medium saucepan cook beans and onion, covered, in a small amount of *boiling water* for 20 to 25 minutes or until tender. Drain.

3. Add Canadian-style bacon or ham, tomato, basil, and pepper to beans in saucepan. Toss lightly. Heat through.

Squeaky-Clean Fruits And Vegetables

When you bring produce home from the grocery store or a farmer's market, follow these tips for removing dirt and pesticide residues:
- Rinse all produce under cold running water. Do not use soap.
- Remove and discard the outer leaves of greens, cabbage, and Brussels sprouts.
- Trim any bruised, wilted, discolored, and tough parts.
- Peel firm vegetables and fruits, such as carrots and potatoes, or scrub them with a soft vegetable brush under running water.

TWICE-BAKED POTATOES

MAKES 4 SERVINGS   PREP: 15 MINUTES   BAKE: 55 MINUTES

2 large baking potatoes
   (7 to 8 ounces each)
2 tablespoons snipped chives
2 tablespoons fat-free dairy sour
   cream French onion dip
   Dash pepper
1 to 2 tablespoons skim milk
2 teaspoons grated Parmesan
   cheese

1. Scrub potatoes thoroughly with a brush. Pat dry with paper towels. Prick potatoes with a fork. Bake in a 425° oven for 40 to 50 minutes or until tender.

2. Cut each potato in half lengthwise. Gently scoop pulp out of each potato half, leaving a thin shell. Place pulp in a medium mixing bowl. Set potato shells aside.

3. With an electric mixer on low speed or a potato masher, beat or mash potato pulp. Add chives, French onion dip, and pepper. Beat until smooth. Beat in enough of the milk to make of desired consistency.

4. Spoon mashed potatoes into potato shells, mounding them slightly. Sprinkle with Parmesan cheese. Place in shallow baking pan. Bake in a 425° oven for about 15 minutes or until heated through and lightly browned.

Make-Ahead Twice-Baked Potatoes: Prepare potatoes as directed above, except after filling potato skins with mashed potato mixture, cover and refrigerate for 4 to 24 hours. Before serving, place chilled potatoes in a shallow baking pan. Bake in a 350° oven about 25 minutes or until heated through and lightly browned.

Fat-free onion dip allows you to add this classic side dish to your list of "can haves."

EXCHANGES
1½ STARCH

NUTRITION FACTS PER SERVING

		Daily Values
Calories	117	5%
Total fat	0 g	0%
Saturated fat	0 g	1%
Cholesterol	1 mg	0%
Sodium	34 mg	1%
Carbohydrate	25 g	8%
Fiber	1 g	3%
Protein	4 g	

BAKED POTATO FRIES

MAKES 4 SERVINGS   PREP: 12 MINUTES   BAKE: 30 MINUTES

2 medium potatoes
   (12 ounces total)
2 teaspoons cooking oil
¼ teaspoon salt
¼ teaspoon paprika

1. Cut each potato lengthwise into 8 wedges.

2. Place potato wedges in a plastic bag; add cooking oil, salt, and paprika. Close bag and shake to coat.

3. On a large baking sheet arrange the potato wedges in a single layer. Bake in a 425° oven for 30 to 35 minutes or until golden brown, turning once or twice.

Cheese Potato Fries: Prepare potatoes as directed above, except omit the salt and paprika; add 1 tablespoon grated *Parmesan cheese*, ¼ teaspoon *garlic powder*, and ¼ teaspoon *pepper* to the potatoes along with the oil.

Chili Fries: Prepare potatoes as directed above, except omit the paprika and add 1 teaspoon *chili powder*; ¼ teaspoon *dried oregano*, crushed; and ⅛ teaspoon *ground cumin* to the potatoes along with the cooking oil.

French fries can now be enjoyed again! Just bake them instead of messy, deep-fat frying them.

EXCHANGES
1 STARCH
½ FAT

NUTRITION FACTS PER SERVING

		Daily Values
Calories	99	4%
Total fat	2 g	3%
Saturated fat	0 g	1%
Cholesterol	0 mg	0%
Sodium	139 mg	5%
Carbohydrate	18 g	6%
Fiber	1 g	2%
Protein	2 g	

PEPPER CORN BREAD

MAKES 10 SERVINGS   PREP: 10 MINUTES   BAKE: 20 MINUTES

Get a double corn flavor from the cornmeal and kernel corn. Serve this spunky bread (pictured on page 79) with chili or stew.

EXCHANGES
2 STARCH

NUTRITION FACTS PER SERVING		
		Daily Values
Calories	149	7%
Total fat	3 g	4%
Saturated fat	1 g	3%
Cholesterol	3 mg	0%
Sodium	298 mg	12%
Carbohydrate	27 g	8%
Fiber	2 g	6%
Protein	5 g	

Nonstick spray coating
1 cup yellow cornmeal
¾ cup all-purpose flour
2 tablespoons sugar
1½ teaspoons baking powder
¼ teaspoon baking soda
¼ teaspoon salt
¼ teaspoon ground red pepper
¾ cup buttermilk
¼ cup refrigerated or frozen egg product, thawed
1 tablespoon cooking oil
1 11-ounce can whole kernel corn with sweet peppers, drained
¼ cup shredded reduced-fat sharp cheddar cheese (1 ounce)
Cornmeal (optional)

1. Spray a 9×1½-inch round baking pan with nonstick coating. Set aside.

2. In a large mixing bowl stir together the 1 cup cornmeal, the flour, sugar, baking powder, baking soda, salt, and ground red pepper. In a medium bowl stir together buttermilk, egg product, and oil. Add to flour mixture. Stir just until moistened. Stir in corn and cheese. Spread into prepared pan. If desired, sprinkle with additional cornmeal. Bake in a 425° oven about 20 minutes or until golden brown. Serve warm or cool.

YOGURT DROP BISCUITS

MAKES 12 BISCUITS   PREP: 10 MINUTES   BAKE: 10 MINUTES

Part of the fat in these flaky biscuits is replaced with low-fat yogurt, cutting the fat by about 6 grams per biscuit.

EXCHANGES
1 STARCH
½ FAT

NUTRITION FACTS PER BISCUIT		
		Daily Values
Calories	114	5%
Total fat	4 g	5%
Saturated fat	1 g	4%
Cholesterol	1 mg	0%
Sodium	151 mg	6%
Carbohydrate	17 g	5%
Fiber	1 g	2%
Protein	3 g	

2 cups all-purpose flour
1 tablespoon baking powder
2 teaspoons sugar
¼ teaspoon salt
3 tablespoons butter-flavored shortening
⅔ cup skim milk
⅔ cup plain low-fat yogurt

1. In a mixing bowl stir together flour, baking powder, sugar, and salt. Cut in shortening until mixture resembles coarse crumbs. Make a well in the center. Add milk and yogurt all at once. Stir just until moistened.

2. Lightly grease a baking sheet. Drop dough by ¼ cupfuls onto prepared baking sheet. Bake in a 450° oven for 10 to 12 minutes or until light brown. Immediately remove biscuits from baking sheet. Cool slightly on wire rack. Serve warm.

DESSERTS

■ STARCH/BREAD   ■ MEAT   ■ FRUIT   ■ VEGETABLE   ■ MILK   ■ FAT

On left: *Strawberry Bavarian Pie, page 82*

STRAWBERRY BAVARIAN PIE

MAKES 10 SERVINGS   PREP: 25 MINUTES   CHILL: 2½ HOURS

Naturally low-fat ladyfinger sponge cakes form the crust for this light, strawberry-flavored pie. Shop for soft ladyfingers at bakeries or grocery stores; the crispy ones will not work as well. (Pie pictured on page 80.)

EXCHANGES
1 STARCH

NUTRITION FACTS PER SERVING

		Daily Values
Calories	98	4%
Total fat	2 g	3%
Saturated fat	2 g	8%
Cholesterol	31 mg	10%
Sodium	39 mg	1%
Carbohydrate	16 g	5%
Fiber	1 g	3%
Protein	3 g	

3 cups fresh strawberries
¼ cup sugar
1 envelope unflavored gelatin
3 slightly beaten egg whites
1 3-ounce package ladyfingers, split
2 tablespoons orange juice
½ of an 8-ounce container frozen light whipped dessert topping, thawed (about 1⅔ cups)
Frozen light whipped dessert topping, thawed (optional)
Fresh strawberries (optional)

1. Place 3 cups strawberries in blender container or food processor bowl. Cover and blend or process until smooth. Measure the strawberries. You should have about 1¾ cups.

2. In a medium saucepan combine sugar and gelatin. Stir in blended strawberries. Cook and stir over medium heat until mixture bubbles and gelatin is dissolved.

3. Gradually stir about half of the gelatin mixture into the slightly beaten egg whites. Return all to the saucepan. Cook, stirring constantly, over low heat for 2 to 3 minutes or until slightly thickened. Do not boil. Pour into a mixing bowl. Chill just until mixture mounds, stirring occasionally.

4. Meanwhile, cut about *half* of the split ladyfingers in half crosswise; stand these on end around the outside edge of a 9- or 9½-inch tart pan with removable bottom or a 9-inch springform pan. Arrange the remaining split ladyfingers in the bottom of the pan. Slowly drizzle the orange juice over the ladyfingers.

5. Fold the whipped topping into the strawberry mixture; spoon into the ladyfinger-lined pan. Cover and refrigerate at least 2 hours or until set. If desired, garnish with dollops of additional whipped topping and strawberries.

Keeping Eggs Safe

Eggs, like any perishable food, need special handling. To make sure your egg dishes are safe and good for you, read the following guidelines.

Safe Handling
■ Purchase clean, fresh eggs from refrigerated display cases.
■ At home, refrigerate eggs promptly in their original carton. Do not wash eggs before storing or using.
■ Discard eggs with cracked shells.
■ For the best quality, use refrigerated raw eggs within a week. You can store

them safely, however, for as long as five weeks. Use leftover yolks and whites within four days and refrigerated hard-cooked eggs within a week.
■ Don't keep eggs out of the refrigerator for more than two hours, including those for a springtime egg hunt.

Smart Cooking, Storing
■ Serve hot egg dishes right away.
■ Refrigerate chilled dishes containing eggs immediately after mixing.
■ Chill egg-based leftovers promptly. Serve within three or four days.

Caution in Cooking
Using uncooked or slightly cooked eggs in recipes for mayonnaise, meringue pies, or Caesar salad can be hazardous, especially to people vulnerable to salmonella—the elderly, infants, children, pregnant women, and the seriously ill. Commercial forms of these foods are safe because they are made with pasteurized eggs. The pasteurization process destroys salmonella bacteria.

PEACH MERINGUE TORTE

MAKES 10 SERVINGS   PREP: 35 MINUTES   BAKE: 30 MINUTES   COOL: 2 HOURS

Nonstick spray coating
½ cup granulated sugar
⅓ cup water
¼ cup almond paste
  Dash salt
⅔ cup sifted cake flour
6 egg whites
  Powdered sugar
2 cups chopped, peeled fresh
    peaches or one 16-ounce
    package frozen unsweetened
    peach slices, thawed and
    chopped
¼ cup granulated sugar
1 tablespoon cornstarch
½ cup granulated sugar
3 egg whites
¼ teaspoon almond extract
¼ teaspoon cream of tartar

1. Spray two 9×1½-inch round baking pans lightly with nonstick coating. Line the bottoms of pans with parchment paper or waxed paper rounds. Set aside.

2. In a food processor bowl or blender container, combine the ½ cup granulated sugar, the water, almond paste, and salt. Cover and blend or process until mixture is smooth. Pour into a medium mixing bowl. Stir in cake flour.

3. In a large mixing bowl beat the 6 egg whites on high speed of an electric mixer until stiff peaks form (tips stand straight). Gently fold about 1 cup of the beaten egg whites into the almond paste mixture. Fold almond paste mixture into remaining egg whites. Spread egg mixture in the prepared pans. Bake cake in a 325° oven for 15 to 18 minutes or until the cake feels firm when lightly touched near the center.

4. Immediately loosen edges of cakes from pans and turn cakes out onto towels or parchment paper sprinkled with powdered sugar. Remove rounds of parchment or waxed paper from cake bottoms. Cool completely.

5. Meanwhile, for filling, in a food processor bowl or blender container, combine *half* of the peaches, the ¼ cup granulated sugar, and the cornstarch. Cover and blend or process until smooth. Pour into a small saucepan. Cook and stir until thickened and bubbly. Cook and stir for 2 minutes more. Stir in remaining peaches.

6. Place a cake layer on an ovenproof serving plate. Spread the peach mixture over this cake layer. Top with the second cake layer.

7. For meringue, in the top of a double boiler combine ½ cup granulated sugar, the 3 egg whites, almond extract, and cream of tartar. Beat with an electric mixer on low speed for 30 seconds. Place over *boiling water* (upper pan should not touch water). Cook, beating constantly with the electric mixer on high speed, about 7 minutes or until stiff peaks form.

8. Spread meringue mixture over top and sides of cake. Bake in a 350° oven for 15 minutes. Cool completely.

Almond paste should be firm but still pliable. If yours is hard, soften it by heating it for 2 to 3 seconds in the microwave oven.

EXCHANGES

| 2 STARCH |
| ½ FRUIT |

NUTRITION FACTS PER SERVING		
		Daily Values
Calories	182	9%
Total fat	2 g	2%
Saturated fat	0 g	0%
Cholesterol	0 mg	0%
Sodium	64 mg	2%
Carbohydrate	38 g	12%
Fiber	1 g	2%
Protein	5 g	

SUMMER FRUIT TART

| MAKES 10 SERVINGS | PREP: 35 MINUTES | BAKE: 10 MINUTES | COOL: 1 HOUR | CHILL: 1 HOUR |

1¼ cups all-purpose flour
¼ teaspoon salt
¼ cup shortening
4 to 5 tablespoons cold water
¼ cup sugar
2 tablespoons cornstarch
1 12-ounce can evaporated
    skim milk
¼ cup refrigerated or frozen egg
    product, thawed
½ teaspoon vanilla
2 medium fresh nectarines or
    peeled peaches, thinly sliced
2 fresh plums, thinly sliced
2 kiwifruit, peeled and sliced
½ cup fresh blueberries,
    raspberries, and/or
    blackberries
2 tablespoons honey
1 tablespoon rum or orange juice

1. In a medium bowl stir together flour and salt. Cut in shortening until mixture resembles fine crumbs. Sprinkle *1 tablespoon* of the water over part of mixture; gently toss with fork. Repeat until all is moistened. Form into ball. On a lightly floured surface, flatten dough. Roll out dough to form a circle about 13 inches in diameter. Ease pastry into 11-inch tart pan with removable bottom, being careful not to stretch pastry. Trim even with edge of pan. Prick pastry well with a fork. Bake in 450° oven for 10 to 12 minutes or until golden brown. Cool completely.

2. For filling, in a heavy medium saucepan combine sugar and cornstarch; stir in the evaporated skim milk and egg product. Cook and stir over medium heat until mixture is thickened and bubbly. Cook and stir for 2 minutes more. Remove from heat. Stir in vanilla. Cover surface with plastic wrap and refrigerate until thoroughly chilled.

3. Spread cooled filling in tart shell. Arrange nectarines, plums, and kiwifruit atop filling. Sprinkle with berries. Mix honey and rum or orange juice; brush on fruit. Cover and refrigerate up to 1 hour. To serve, remove side of pan.

A pudding-like mixture fills this fruit-topped tart (pictured on page 84). Use any type of in-season fruit you like.

EXCHANGES

| 1 STARCH |
| 1 FRUIT |
| 1 FAT |

NUTRITION FACTS PER SERVING

		Daily Values
Calories	187	9%
Total fat	6 g	9%
Saturated fat	1 g	5%
Cholesterol	1 mg	0%
Sodium	84 mg	4%
Carbohydrate	31 g	10%
Fiber	2 g	8%
Protein	4 g	

MINT-CHOCOLATE CHIP ICE MILK

| MAKES 16 SERVINGS | PREP: 15 MINUTES | CHILL: 1 HOUR | FREEZE: 30 MINUTES |

¾ cup sugar
1 envelope unflavored gelatin
1 12-ounce can evaporated
    skim milk
1 egg
1 egg white
2½ cups skim milk
2 tablespoons crème de menthe or
¼ teaspoon mint extract
2 teaspoons vanilla
    Several drops green food
    coloring (optional)
1½ ounces semisweet chocolate,
    chopped

1. In a large saucepan stir together the sugar and gelatin. Stir in evaporated skim milk. Cook and stir over medium-low heat until sugar and gelatin dissolve and mixture almost boils. Remove from heat.

2. In a small bowl slightly beat egg and egg white. Stir about ½ cup of the hot gelatin mixture into the egg mixture. Return all to saucepan. Cook and stir over low heat for 2 minutes more. Do not boil.

3. Stir in milk, crème de menthe or mint extract, and vanilla. Cover and refrigerate until thoroughly chilled.

4. If desired, stir food coloring into cooled mixture. Stir in semisweet chocolate. Freeze in a 4- to 5-quart ice-cream freezer according to manufacturer's directions.

Imagine being able to enjoy mint-flavored chocolate chip ice cream for less than 96 calories a serving. Heavenly!

EXCHANGES

| ½ STARCH |
| ½ MILK |

NUTRITION FACTS PER ½-CUP SERVING

		Daily Values
Calories	96	4%
Total fat	1 g	1%
Saturated fat	1 g	3%
Cholesterol	15 mg	4%
Sodium	53 mg	2%
Carbohydrate	16 g	5%
Fiber	0 g	0%
Protein	4 g	

CHEESECAKES WITH APRICOT SAUCE

MAKES 6 SERVINGS   PREP: 20 MINUTES   BAKE: 15 MINUTES   CHILL: 2 TO 24 HOURS

These great little cheesecakes make the perfect ending to a company meal.

EXCHANGES

| 1 FRUIT |
| 1 MILK |
| 1 FAT |

NUTRITION FACTS PER SERVING

		Daily Values
Calories	191	9%
Total fat	10 g	14%
Saturated fat	6 g	28%
Cholesterol	29 mg	9%
Sodium	189 mg	7%
Carbohydrate	19 g	6%
Fiber	1 g	2%
Protein	7 g	

1 8-ounce package reduced-fat cream cheese (Neufchâtel), softened
¼ cup sugar
½ teaspoon vanilla
  Dash ground nutmeg
½ cup refrigerated or frozen egg product, thawed
2 teaspoons sugar
2 teaspoons cornstarch
1 5½-ounce can apricot or peach nectar
1 tablespoon amaretto or orange juice
4 apricots, thinly sliced, or 2 medium nectarines or peeled peaches, thinly sliced
8 fresh mint leaves (optional)

1. Line six 6-ounce custard cups with paper bake cups. Set aside.

2. In a medium mixing bowl beat together the cream cheese, sugar, vanilla, and nutmeg with an electric mixer on low to medium speed. Add the egg product; beat on low speed until smooth. Pour into prepared cups. Place cups in a shallow baking pan.

3. Bake in a 325° oven for 15 to 20 minutes or until the center is just set. Remove from cups. Cool on a wire rack for 15 minutes. Cover and refrigerate for 2 to 24 hours.

4. For sauce, in a small saucepan combine sugar and cornstarch. Stir in nectar and amaretto or orange juice. Cook and stir over medium heat until thickened and bubbly. Cook and stir for 2 minutes more. Stir in fruit.

5. Before serving, invert cheesecakes onto individual dessert plates. Remove papers. Spoon sauce over cheesecakes. If desired, garnish with mint leaves.

STRAWBERRY FROZEN DESSERT

MAKES 14 SERVINGS   PREP: 45 MINUTES   CHILL: 30 MINUTES   FREEZE: 25 MINUTES

If you thought enjoying strawberry ice cream was a thing of the past, pinch yourself, then have a bite of pure berry pleasure.

EXCHANGES

| 1 FRUIT |
| ½ MILK |

NUTRITION FACTS PER ½-CUP SERVING

		Daily Values
Calories	88	4%
Total fat	0 g	0%
Saturated fat	0 g	0%
Cholesterol	1 mg	0%
Sodium	44 mg	1%
Carbohydrate	20 g	6%
Fiber	3 g	12%
Protein	3 g	

¼ cup sugar
2 tablespoons cornstarch
1 teaspoon finely shredded lemon peel
2 cups evaporated skim milk
1½ teaspoons vanilla
2 10-ounce packages frozen strawberries in syrup, thawed
1 tablespoon lemon juice
  Fresh strawberries (optional)
  Fresh mint leaves (optional)

1. In a small saucepan stir together sugar, cornstarch, and lemon peel. Stir in evaporated skim milk. Cook and stir until thickened and bubbly. Cook and stir for 2 minutes more. Stir in the vanilla. Cover and refrigerate for at least 30 minutes.

2. In a blender container or food processor bowl, combine strawberries in syrup and lemon juice. Cover and blend or process until smooth.

3. Stir strawberry mixture into chilled milk mixture. Freeze in a 2- to 3-quart ice-cream freezer according to the manufacturer's directions. Scoop into serving dishes. If desired, garnish with fresh berries and mint leaves.

OATMEAL-APPLESAUCE CAKE

MAKES 20 SERVINGS   PREP: 15 MINUTES   BAKE: 25 MINUTES   COOL: 1 HOUR

Nonstick spray coating
2 cups all-purpose flour
⅔ cup quick-cooking rolled oats
2 teaspoons baking powder
½ teaspoon baking soda
½ teaspoon ground cinnamon
¼ teaspoon salt
⅛ teaspoon ground nutmeg
1 cup packed brown sugar
⅓ cup margarine or butter, softened
1¾ cups applesauce
¼ cup refrigerated or frozen egg product, thawed
1 teaspoon vanilla
¾ cup raisins or dried mixed fruit bits
1 tablespoon sifted powdered sugar

1. Spray a 13×9×2-inch baking pan with nonstick coating. Set aside. In a mixing bowl stir together the flour, oats, baking powder, baking soda, cinnamon, salt, and nutmeg. Set aside.

2. In a large mixing bowl combine brown sugar and margarine or butter. Beat with an electric mixer on medium speed until combined. Add applesauce, egg product, and vanilla. Beat until well mixed. Add flour mixture; beat until combined. Stir in raisins or fruit bits.

3. Spread into prepared pan. Bake in a 350° oven for 25 to 30 minutes or until a wooden toothpick inserted near center comes out clean. Cool completely in pan on a wire rack. Sprinkle with powdered sugar.

Reduce the fat in this spicy, fruit-filled cake to just 4 grams by using powdered sugar instead of frosting, replacing some of the fat with applesauce, and using fat-free egg product.

EXCHANGES

| 1 STARCH |
| 1 FRUIT |
| ½ FAT |

NUTRITION FACTS PER SERVING

		Daily Values
Calories	151	7%
Total fat	4 g	5%
Saturated fat	1 g	3%
Cholesterol	0 mg	0%
Sodium	140 mg	5%
Carbohydrate	29 g	9%
Fiber	1 g	4%
Protein	2 g	

FRUIT AMBROSIA

MAKES 6 SERVINGS   PREP: 15 MINUTES   CHILL: 1 TO 6 HOURS

1 8-ounce can pineapple tidbits, drained
1 cup fresh halved strawberries, raspberries, or pitted sweet cherries
1 cup seedless green grapes, halved
½ cup tiny marshmallows
½ of an 8-ounce carton lemon or orange fat-free yogurt
¼ of an 8-ounce container frozen light whipped dessert topping, thawed (scant 1 cup)

1. In a mixing bowl combine pineapple; strawberries, raspberries, or cherries; grapes; and marshmallows.

2. In another bowl fold together yogurt and whipped topping. Gently fold into fruit mixture. Cover and refrigerate for 1 to 6 hours. Before serving, spoon into individual dessert dishes.

Ambrosia was the food of the gods in ancient Greece. The word now describes a fruit mixture that is usually topped with coconut.

EXCHANGES

| 1½ FRUIT |
| ½ FAT |

NUTRITION FACTS PER SERVING

		Daily Values
Calories	115	5%
Total fat	3 g	4%
Saturated fat	2 g	11%
Cholesterol	1 mg	0%
Sodium	31 mg	1%
Carbohydrate	23 g	7%
Fiber	1 g	4%
Protein	1 g	

LEMON BARS WITH RASPBERRIES

MAKES 18 SERVINGS   PREP: 25 MINUTES   BAKE: 35 MINUTES   COOL: 1 HOUR

Impressive and easy to make, this refreshingly tart dessert is a great ending for any meal (pictured on page 89).

EXCHANGES

1 STARCH
½ FAT

NUTRITION FACTS PER SERVING

		Daily Values
Calories	96	5%
Total fat	3 g	5%
Saturated fat	1 g	5%
Cholesterol	12 mg	4%
Sodium	42 mg	2%
Carbohydrate	17 g	6%
Fiber	1 g	4%
Protein	1 g	

Nonstick spray coating
¾ cup all-purpose flour
3 tablespoons sugar
¼ cup margarine or butter
1 egg
1 egg white
⅔ cup sugar
2 tablespoons all-purpose flour
1 teaspoon finely shredded lemon peel (set aside)
2 tablespoons lemon juice
1 tablespoon water
¼ teaspoon baking powder
1½ cups fresh raspberries
2 tablespoons red currant jelly, melted

1. Spray an 8×8×2-inch baking pan with nonstick coating. Set aside. In a small mixing bowl combine the ¾ cup flour and the 3 tablespoons sugar. Cut in margarine or butter until crumbly. Pat mixture onto the bottom of the prepared pan. Bake in a 350° oven for 15 minutes.

2. For filling, in a small mixing bowl combine egg and egg white. Beat with an electric mixer on medium speed until frothy. Add the ⅔ cup sugar, the 2 tablespoons flour, the lemon juice, water, and baking powder. Beat on medium speed for 3 minutes or until slightly thickened. Stir in lemon peel. Pour over hot baked layer in pan. Bake in a 350° oven for 20 to 25 minutes more or until edges are light brown and center is set. Cool completely in pan on a wire rack. Cut into 9 squares; cut each square diagonally to make a triangle. Top triangles with raspberries. Drizzle with the jelly.

SWEET TOPPED BERRIES

MAKES 4 SERVINGS   PREP: 15 MINUTES

Berries and cream don't have to be taken off your menu. Just make sure the whipped "cream" is low in fat, as this one is.

EXCHANGES

1 FRUIT
½ FAT

NUTRITION FACTS PER SERVING

		Daily Values
Calories	94	4%
Total fat	3 g	4%
Saturated fat	2 g	10%
Cholesterol	1 mg	0%
Sodium	24 mg	0%
Carbohydrate	16 g	5%
Fiber	2 g	8%
Protein	1 g	

½ teaspoon finely shredded orange peel
2 tablespoons orange juice
2 cups fresh raspberries, blueberries, and/or sliced strawberries
¼ of an 8-ounce container frozen light whipped dessert topping, thawed (scant 1 cup)
⅓ cup vanilla low-fat yogurt
1 tablespoon orange, raspberry, or almond liqueur or orange juice
Finely shredded orange peel (optional)

1. In a medium bowl stir together the ½ teaspoon orange peel and the 2 tablespoons orange juice.

2. Add berries. Toss to coat.

3. For topping, in a small mixing bowl fold together whipped topping, yogurt, and the 1 tablespoon liqueur or orange juice.

4. Divide fruit mixture among 4 dessert dishes. Spoon some of the topping over each serving. If desired, sprinkle with additional shredded orange peel. Serve immediately.

LEMON CAKE

MAKES 12 SERVINGS   PREP: 20 MINUTES   BAKE: 30 MINUTES   COOL: 30 MINUTES

Lemon syrup adds an extra lemony flavor to this cake. Make it with or without berries.

EXCHANGES

2 STARCH
½ FAT

NUTRITION FACTS PER SERVING FOR LEMON CAKE

		Daily Values
Calories	178	9%
Total fat	4 g	6%
Saturated fat	1 g	5%
Cholesterol	1 mg	0%
Sodium	224 mg	9%
Carbohydrate	34 g	11%
Fiber	0 g	0%
Protein	3 g	

EXCHANGES

2 STARCH
½ FAT

NUTRITION FACTS PER SERVING FOR LEMON-BERRY CAKE

		Daily Values
Calories	184	9%
Total fat	4 g	6%
Saturated fat	1 g	5%
Cholesterol	1 mg	0%
Sodium	225 mg	9%
Carbohydrate	35 g	12%
Fiber	1 g	4%
Protein	3 g	

Nonstick spray coating
2 teaspoons all-purpose flour
1½ cups all-purpose flour
2 teaspoons baking powder
½ teaspoon baking soda
¼ teaspoon salt
1 cup granulated sugar
½ cup refrigerated or frozen egg product, thawed
⅔ cup buttermilk
3 tablespoons margarine or butter
2 teaspoons finely shredded lemon peel (set aside)
1 tablespoon lemon juice
1 teaspoon vanilla
1 recipe Lemon Syrup
1 tablespoon sifted powdered sugar

1. Spray an 8-inch fluted tube pan with nonstick coating. Sprinkle with the 2 teaspoons flour. Shake pan to coat with flour. Set aside. In a mixing bowl stir together the 1½ cups flour, baking powder, soda, and salt. Set aside.

2. In a medium mixing bowl gradually add granulated sugar to egg product, beating with an electric mixer on medium to high speed about 4 minutes or until thick and light.

3. Add flour mixture, beating on low speed just until combined (batter will be thick).

4. In a small saucepan combine buttermilk and margarine or butter. Heat and stir over medium heat until margarine or butter melts. Add to batter along with lemon juice and vanilla. Beat on low speed just until combined. Stir in peel. Pour into prepared pan. Bake in a 350° oven for 30 to 40 minutes or until a wooden toothpick inserted near center comes out clean. Cool in pan on a wire rack for 10 minutes. Remove cake from pan. Cool slightly.

5. With a wooden skewer, cake tester or long-tined fork, poke holes over the surface of the cake. While the cake is still warm, slowly drizzle Lemon Syrup over cake. Sprinkle with powdered sugar. Serve warm* or cooled.

Lemon Syrup: Stir together ½ cup sifted *powdered sugar* and 2 tablespoons *lemon juice*.

Lemon-Berry Cake: Prepare cake as directed above, except just before pouring into pan fold ¾ cup fresh or frozen *blueberries* or *raspberries* into the batter. If using frozen fruit, increase baking time to 35 to 45 minutes.

*Note: If desired, cake may be rewarmed in microwave oven (on a microwave-safe plate) on 50% power (medium) for 1½ to 2 minutes or just until warm.

CHERRY BROWNIES

MAKES 16 SERVINGS   PREP: 20 MINUTES   BAKE: 15 MINUTES   COOL: 1 HOUR   STAND: 30 MINUTES

Nonstick spray coating
¾ cup all-purpose flour
¾ cup granulated sugar
¼ cup unsweetened cocoa powder
½ teaspoon baking powder
¼ teaspoon salt
½ cup refrigerated or frozen egg product, thawed
¼ cup cooking oil
1 teaspoon vanilla
1 cup frozen pitted tart red cherries, thawed and drained, or ½ of a 16-ounce can pitted tart red cherries, drained
1 recipe Chocolate Glaze or sifted powdered sugar

1. Spray the bottom of an 8×8×2-inch baking pan with nonstick coating. Set aside.

2. In a large mixing bowl stir together the flour, granulated sugar, cocoa powder, baking powder, and salt. Make a well in the center. Add the egg product, oil, and vanilla. Beat with a spoon until well mixed. Spread in the prepared baking pan. Sprinkle cherries on top.

3. Bake in a 350° oven about 15 minutes or until top springs back when lightly touched. Cool completely in pan on a wire rack. Drizzle with the Chocolate Glaze or sprinkle with powdered sugar. Let stand about 30 minutes or until glaze is set. Cut into bars.

Chocolate Glaze: In a small mixing bowl stir together ⅓ cup sifted *powdered sugar*, 1 tablespoon *unsweetened cocoa powder*, and 2 to 3 teaspoons *milk* to make of drizzling consistency.

Borrowing the cherry-chocolate flavor combination from the famous Black Forest Torte, these tasty brownies will cure sweet-tooth cravings but only add 114 calories to your daily total.

EXCHANGES

1 STARCH
½ FAT

NUTRITION FACTS PER SERVING

		Daily Values
Calories	114	5%
Total fat	4 g	6%
Saturated fat	1 g	2%
Cholesterol	0 mg	0%
Sodium	59 mg	2%
Carbohydrate	18 g	5%
Fiber	0 g	1%
Protein	2 g	

FRESH FRUIT PLATE

MAKES 4 SERVINGS   PREP: 15 MINUTES

¼ of an 8-ounce package reduced-fat cream cheese (Neufchâtel), softened
½ of an 8-ounce carton peach, lemon, orange, or pineapple low-fat yogurt (scant ½ cup)
1 tablespoon orange juice
½ teaspoon vanilla
4 cups fresh sliced strawberries, sliced peeled kiwifruit, and/or raspberries
Fresh mint leaves (optional)

1. In a small mixing bowl beat cream cheese with electric mixer on low speed until smooth. Add yogurt, orange juice, and vanilla. Beat on low speed until combined. Spoon one-fourth of the cream cheese mixture onto each of 4 dessert plates. Arrange 1 cup of fruit on each plate. If desired, garnish with mint leaves.

This fruit dish is like eating soft cheesecake with a spoon.

EXCHANGES

1 FRUIT
½ FAT

NUTRITION FACTS PER SERVING

		Daily Values
Calories	114	5%
Total fat	4 g	6%
Saturated fat	2 g	11%
Cholesterol	12 mg	4%
Sodium	75 mg	3%
Carbohydrate	17 g	5%
Fiber	3 g	11%
Protein	4 g	

MINT-CHOCOLATE CREAM PUFFS

MAKES 8 SERVINGS   PREP: 25 MINUTES   BAKE: 30 MINUTES   COOL: 1 HOUR

Nonstick spray coating
½ **cup water**
2 **tablespoons margarine or butter**
½ **cup all-purpose flour**
2 **eggs**
1 **4-serving-size package fat-free** *instant* **chocolate pudding mix or reduced-calorie** *regular* **chocolate pudding mix**
⅛ **teaspoon peppermint extract**
1 **cup sliced fresh strawberries**

1. Spray a baking sheet with nonstick coating. Set aside.

2. In a small saucepan combine the water and margarine or butter. Bring to boiling. Add flour all at once, stirring vigorously. Cook and stir until mixture forms a ball that doesn't separate. Remove from heat. Cool for 5 minutes. Add eggs, *one* at a time, beating after each addition until mixture is shiny and smooth. Drop mixture in 8 mounds 3 inches apart on the prepared baking sheet.

3. Bake in a 400° oven about 30 minutes or until golden brown. Remove from oven. Split puffs and remove any soft dough from inside. Cool completely on a wire rack.

4. Meanwhile, for filling, prepare pudding mix according to package directions. Stir in peppermint extract. Cover surface with plastic wrap. Refrigerate the filling until thoroughly chilled.

5. To serve, spoon about ¼ cup of the filling into the bottom half of each cream puff. Top with sliced strawberries. Replace tops.

Watching your diet doesn't mean giving up chocolate. These minty chocolate puffs have loads of flavor and only 126 calories per serving (pictured on page 92).

EXCHANGES

1½ STARCH
½ FAT

NUTRITION FACTS PER SERVING

		Daily Values
Calories	126	6%
Total fat	4 g	6%
Saturated fat	1 g	5%
Cholesterol	53 mg	18%
Sodium	225 mg	9%
Carbohydrate	20 g	7%
Fiber	1 g	4%
Protein	2 g	

CITRUS SHERBET

MAKES 16 SERVINGS   PREP: 15 MINUTES   COOL: 20 MINUTES   FREEZE: 30 MINUTES

1½ **cups sugar**
1 **envelope unflavored gelatin**
3½ **cups orange juice**
1 **cup buttermilk**
1 **teaspoon finely shredded lime peel or lemon peel**
¼ **cup lime juice or lemon juice**

1. In a medium saucepan stir together sugar and gelatin. Stir in orange juice. Cook and stir over medium heat until sugar and gelatin dissolve. Remove from heat. Cool slightly. Stir in buttermilk, lime or lemon peel, and lime or lemon juice.

2. Freeze in a 4- or 5-quart ice cream freezer according to the manufacturer's directions.

Just a few healthful ingredients and you're on your way to a great-tasting dessert.

EXCHANGES

1½ FRUIT

NUTRITION FACTS PER ½-CUP SERVING

		Daily Values
Calories	106	5%
Total fat	0 g	0%
Saturated fat	0 g	0%
Cholesterol	1 mg	0%
Sodium	17 mg	0%
Carbohydrate	25 g	8%
Fiber	0 g	1%
Protein	1 g	

SNACKS & APPETIZERS

■ STARCH/BREAD   ■ MEAT   ■ VEGETABLE   ■ FRUIT   ■ MILK   ■ FAT

On left: *Gingered Shrimp Appetizers, page 96*

GINGERED SHRIMP APPETIZERS

MAKES 6 TO 8 SERVINGS   PREP: 40 MINUTES   MARINATE: 1 TO 2 HOURS

The lightly steamed pea pods dress up the tangy marinated shrimp, making them an elegant appetizer (pictured on page 94).

EXCHANGES
1½ VERY LEAN MEAT

NUTRITION FACTS PER SERVING

		Daily Values
Calories	60	3%
Total fat	1 g	1%
Saturated fat	0 g	1%
Cholesterol	87 mg	29%
Sodium	123 mg	5%
Carbohydrate	2 g	0%
Fiber	1 g	2%
Protein	10 g	

1 pound fresh or frozen large shrimp in shells
1½ cups water
4½ teaspoons white wine vinegar
1 teaspoon toasted sesame oil or olive oil
¼ teaspoon finely shredded lemon peel
1 teaspoon lemon juice
1 teaspoon grated gingerroot or ½ teaspoon ground ginger
¼ teaspoon sugar
Dash salt
Dash ground red pepper
1 clove garlic, minced
18 to 24 fresh pea pods
6 to 8 small pieces lemon

1. Thaw shrimp, if frozen. Peel and devein shrimp, leaving the last few sections before the tails and the tails intact. In a large saucepan bring the water to boiling. Add the shrimp. Cover and simmer for 1 to 3 minutes or until the shrimp turn opaque. Drain. Rinse the shrimp with cold water; drain.

2. Place shrimp in a plastic bag set in a shallow bowl. Add the vinegar, oil, lemon peel, lemon juice, gingerroot, sugar, salt, ground red pepper, and garlic to bag. Close bag. Marinate in the refrigerator for 1 to 2 hours.

3. Place pea pods in the top of a steamer over *boiling water*. Cover and steam for 2 to 3 minutes or until the pea pods are just tender. Rinse with cold water; drain.

4. Drain shrimp, discarding marinade. Wrap each shrimp with a pea pod. On each of six or eight 6-inch skewers, thread 1 piece of lemon and 3 wrapped shrimp.

VEGGIE QUESADILLAS

MAKES 8 SERVINGS   PREP: 25 MINUTES   BAKE: 5 MINUTES

Vegetables make these quesadillas a snack you can feel good about having. Substitute your favorite vegetables if you like.

EXCHANGES
½ STARCH
1 VEGETABLE
½ FAT

NUTRITION FACTS PER SERVING

		Daily Values
Calories	87	4%
Total fat	3 g	4%
Saturated fat	1 g	4%
Cholesterol	5 mg	1%
Sodium	136 mg	5%
Carbohydrate	12 g	3%
Fiber	1 g	2%
Protein	4 g	

Nonstick spray coating
½ of a medium onion, sliced and separated into rings
½ cup finely chopped broccoli, cauliflower, and/or fresh mushrooms
1 clove garlic, minced
2 tablespoons chopped canned green chili peppers, drained
4 7-inch flour tortillas
½ cup shredded reduced-fat cheddar or Monterey Jack cheese (2 ounces)

1. Spray an unheated large skillet with nonstick coating. Preheat over medium heat. Add onion rings, vegetables, and garlic; cook and stir until tender. Remove from heat. Stir in chili peppers.

2. Place tortillas on a baking sheet. Spoon some of the vegetable mixture over half of each tortilla. Sprinkle with the cheese. Fold remaining half of each tortilla over cheese and vegetables. Bake in a 350° oven about 5 minutes or until cheese melts.

3. To serve, cut each tortilla into 4 wedges.

SALMON SPREAD WITH PITA WEDGES

MAKES 4 SERVINGS   PREP: 25 MINUTES   CHILL: 2 TO 24 HOURS   BAKE: 4 MINUTES

1 6½-ounce can skinless,
    boneless salmon, drained
    and flaked
¼ cup finely chopped celery
2 tablespoons finely chopped
    green onion
3 tablespoons fat-free mayonnaise
    dressing or salad dressing
1 tablespoon Dijon-style mustard
1 teaspoon snipped fresh dill or
    ¼ teaspoon dried dillweed
    Nonstick spray coating
2 small pita bread rounds
4 lettuce leaves

1. In a medium mixing bowl combine salmon, celery, green onion, mayonnaise dressing or salad dressing, mustard, and dill. Mix well. Spray a 1-cup mold or bowl or a 10-ounce custard cup with nonstick coating. Press salmon mixture into the mold, bowl, or custard cup. Cover and refrigerate for 2 to 24 hours.

2. For pita wedges, split each pita bread round horizontally so you have 4 rounds. Cut each round into 8 wedges. Arrange wedges on a baking sheet. Bake in a 450° oven for 4 to 5 minutes or until dry and crisp. Cool.

3. Line a serving plate with lettuce leaves. Run a spatula around edge of mold, bowl, or cup to loosen. Invert onto lettuce-lined plate. Lift and remove mold, bowl, or cup. Serve salmon mixture with pita wedges.

If you're watching your sodium intake, substitute ½ cup flaked, poached salmon steaks for the canned salmon.

EXCHANGES

1 STARCH
1½ LEAN MEAT

NUTRITION FACTS PER SERVING

		Daily Values
Calories	165	8%
Total fat	4 g	5%
Saturated fat	1 g	3%
Cholesterol	25 mg	8%
Sodium	662 mg	27%
Carbohydrate	20 g	6%
Fiber	0 g	1%
Protein	12 g	

BLACK BEAN DIP

MAKES 24 SERVINGS   PREP: 10 MINUTES

1 15-ounce can black beans,
    drained and rinsed
½ cup salsa
2 tablespoons lightly packed fresh
    cilantro or parsley
1 tablespoon lime juice
¼ teaspoon ground cumin
⅛ teaspoon salt
⅛ teaspoon pepper
1 clove garlic, minced
    Baked tortilla chips (optional)*

1. In a blender container or food processor bowl combine beans, salsa, cilantro or parsley, lime juice, cumin, salt, pepper, and garlic. Cover and blend or process until smooth. Serve with baked tortilla chips.

*Note: You may either purchase baked tortilla chips or make your own. To make your own, cut eight 7-inch corn tortillas into 1-inch-wide strips. Spread strips in a single layer on a baking sheet. (You'll need to bake chips in batches.) Bake in a 350° oven for 10 to 12 minutes or until crisp. Makes 8 servings. (Exchanges: 1 Starch)

Simple foods are sometimes the best. Indulge in this bean dip since each tablespoon has only 13 calories.

EXCHANGES

FREE FOOD

NUTRITION FACTS
PER 1-TABLESPOON SERVING

		Daily Values
Calories	13	0%
Total fat	0 g	0%
Saturated fat	0 g	0%
Cholesterol	0 mg	0%
Sodium	73 mg	3%
Carbohydrate	3 g	0%
Fiber	1 g	3%
Protein	1 g	

CURRIED CHEESE VEGETABLES

MAKES 12 SERVINGS   PREP: 25 MINUTES

These colorful vegetable snacks are filled with a curry-spiked cream cheese mixture (pictured on page 99).

EXCHANGES

½ VEGETABLE
½ FAT

NUTRITION FACTS PER SERVING

		Daily Values
Calories	33	1%
Total fat	2 g	3%
Saturated fat	1 g	7%
Cholesterol	7 mg	2%
Sodium	42 mg	1%
Carbohydrate	2 g	0%
Fiber	1 g	2%
Protein	1 g	

24 cherry tomatoes and/or baby pattypan squash and/or 12 baby zucchini
½ of an 8-ounce package reduced-fat cream cheese (Neufchâtel), softened
½ cup finely shredded carrot
2 tablespoons sliced green onion
½ teaspoon curry powder
⅛ teaspoon garlic powder
1 tablespoon skim milk
  Paprika (optional)
  Fresh dill (optional)

1. Cut a thin layer off the stem end of each cherry tomato. Use a melon baller or a small spoon to hollow out the inside of each tomato or pattypan squash. Invert on paper towels. Halve each zucchini; use a melon baller or a small spoon to hollow out each zucchini half. Invert on paper towels. Set aside.

2. In a small mixing bowl stir together cream cheese, carrot, green onion, curry powder, garlic powder, and milk. Spoon mixture into the centers of the hollowed-out vegetables. If desired, sprinkle with paprika and garnish with fresh dill.

PEANUT-PINEAPPLE NIBBLES

MAKES 4 SERVINGS   PREP: 15 MINUTES

Remember celery stuffed with peanut butter? Try our spiced-up version to refresh your memory.

EXCHANGES

½ HIGH-FAT MEAT
½ FRUIT

NUTRITION FACTS PER SERVING

		Daily Values
Calories	78	3%
Total fat	3 g	4%
Saturated fat	1 g	2%
Cholesterol	3 mg	0%
Sodium	62 mg	2%
Carbohydrate	9 g	2%
Fiber	1 g	3%
Protein	5 g	

⅓ of an 8-ounce tub fat-free cream cheese (about ⅓ cup)
2 tablespoons reduced-fat or regular creamy peanut butter
  Dash bottled hot pepper sauce
¼ cup drained crushed pineapple
3 stalks celery, cut into 2-inch pieces

1. In a small mixing bowl stir together cream cheese, peanut butter, and bottled hot pepper sauce until smooth. Stir in crushed pineapple. Spoon the pineapple mixture into the celery pieces.

ROASTED RED PEPPER DIP

MAKES 12 SERVINGS   PREP: 10 MINUTES   CHILL: 4 TO 24 HOURS

If roasted peppers are your passion, you'll love this dip. Use it as a topper for a sandwich instead of mayonnaise. For a 1-tablespoon serving, this is a free food (less than 20 calories).

EXCHANGES
FREE FOOD

NUTRITION FACTS
PER 1-TABLESPOON SERVING DIP

		Daily Values
Calories	19	1%
Total fat	0 g	0%
Saturated fat	0 g	0%
Cholesterol	0 mg	0%
Sodium	23 mg	1%
Carbohydrate	3 g	1%
Fiber	0 g	0%
Protein	1 g	

1   8-ounce carton fat-free dairy sour cream
¼   cup chopped roasted red sweet peppers (about ¼ of a 7-ounce jar)
2   tablespoons sliced green onion
1   teaspoon snipped fresh basil or ¼ teaspoon dried basil, crushed
2   cloves garlic, minced
    Dash salt
    Assorted vegetable dippers or crackers (optional)*

1. In a small mixing bowl stir together sour cream, roasted red peppers, green onion, basil, garlic, and salt. Cover and refrigerate for 4 to 24 hours to allow flavors to blend. Stir before serving. If desired, serve with assorted vegetable dippers or crackers.

*Note: Choose from a 1-cup serving of broccoli flowerets, zucchini, celery, and/or carrot (Exchanges: 1 Vegetable), or 5 whole wheat crackers (Exchanges: 1 Starch).

CURRIED SNACK MIX

MAKES 6 SERVINGS   PREP: 10 MINUTES   BAKE: 20 MINUTES

This easy-to-make snack mix will ease your cravings for something crunchy without adding loads of calories.

EXCHANGES
1 STARCH

NUTRITION FACTS
PER ½-CUP SERVING

		Daily Values
Calories	76	3%
Total fat	2 g	3%
Saturated fat	1 g	2%
Cholesterol	0 mg	0%
Sodium	176 mg	7%
Carbohydrate	12 g	4%
Fiber	0 g	1%
Protein	1 g	

3   plain rice cakes, broken into bite-size pieces
1   cup bite-size square corn cereal or oyster crackers
¾   cup pretzel sticks, halved (1 ounce)
1   tablespoon margarine or butter, melted
1   teaspoon Worcestershire sauce
½   teaspoon curry powder

1. In a 13×9×2-inch baking pan stir together broken rice cakes, corn cereal or oyster crackers, and pretzels.

2. In a custard cup stir together melted margarine or butter, Worcestershire sauce, and curry powder. Drizzle margarine mixture over cereal mixture. Toss cereal mixture until coated. Bake mixture in a 300° oven about 20 minutes, stirring twice. Cool completely. Store in a tightly covered container for up to 1 week.

HAM-FILLED BISCUIT BITES

MAKES 16 SERVINGS   PREP: 15 MINUTES   BAKE: 8 MINUTES

1 cup all-purpose flour
1 teaspoon baking powder
1 teaspoon sugar
⅛ teaspoon baking soda
⅛ teaspoon salt
2 tablespoons cold margarine
　 or butter
½ cup plain fat-free yogurt
½ cup finely chopped lower-fat
　 cooked ham
¼ cup finely chopped, seeded
　 cucumber
2 tablespoons fat-free mayonnaise
　 dressing or salad dressing
2 teaspoons honey mustard
¼ teaspoon dried dillweed
　 Dash pepper

1. For the biscuit bites, in a medium mixing bowl combine the flour, baking powder, sugar, baking soda, and salt. Cut the margarine or butter into flour mixture until mixture resembles coarse crumbs. Make a well in center.

2. Add yogurt; stir just until dough clings together. On a lightly floured surface, knead dough gently for 8 to 10 strokes. Roll or pat dough until about ½ inch thick. Cut with a 1½-inch round cutter. Reroll as necessary to make 16 biscuits.

3. Transfer rounds to an ungreased baking sheet. Bake in a 425° oven for 8 to 10 minutes or until light brown. Remove from baking sheet. Cool slightly on wire rack.

4. Meanwhile, in a small mixing bowl stir together ham, cucumber, mayonnaise dressing or salad dressing, honey mustard, dillweed, and pepper. To serve, split biscuit bites in half. Fill each with some of the ham mixture.

These mini biscuits filled with ham salad are the perfect fare for a casual party.

EXCHANGES

½ STARCH
½ FAT

NUTRITION FACTS PER SERVING

		Daily Values
Calories	52	2%
Total fat	2 g	2%
Saturated fat	0 g	1%
Cholesterol	2 mg	0%
Sodium	152 mg	6%
Carbohydrate	7 g	2%
Fiber	0 g	0%
Protein	2 g	

CHILI POPCORN

MAKES 4 SERVINGS   PREP: 15 MINUTES

2 tablespoons unpopped popcorn
1 teaspoon chili powder
⅛ teaspoon garlic powder
1 tablespoon margarine or butter,
　 melted
2 tablespoons grated Parmesan
　 cheese

1. Pop popcorn with an air popper. (Or, place popcorn in a heavy skillet. Do not add any oil. Cover and pop over medium-high heat, shaking constantly.) This should make about 4 cups popped popcorn.

2. Stir chili powder and garlic powder into the melted margarine or butter. Drizzle over popcorn. Add Parmesan cheese and toss until coated.

A little margarine plus a trio of ingredients with a lot of flavor make ho-hum popcorn great.

EXCHANGES

½ STARCH
1 FAT

NUTRITION FACTS PER 1-CUP SERVING

		Daily Values
Calories	82	4%
Total fat	4 g	6%
Saturated fat	1 g	5%
Cholesterol	2 mg	0%
Sodium	98 mg	4%
Carbohydrate	9 g	2%
Fiber	1 g	4%
Protein	3 g	

HELPING YOUR CHILD GROW UP SLIM

Gone are the days when we believed a chubby child was a healthy child. We now know that an overweight preschooler has an increased risk of remaining fat into adulthood; a teenager runs an even greater risk. Obesity contributes to many health problems, such as heart disease, diabetes, high blood pressure, and weak joints.

Because children and teenagers are continually growing until their late teens, it's important *not* to put children on a restrictive diet. The best thing parents can do for their children is to help them eat moderately and healthfully and encourage physical activity. Keep the cupboards and refrigerator stocked with healthful foods and serve meals low in fat and moderate in calories. You can begin by serving the recipes in this book, which are appropriate for the whole family.* Although you can't police everything your children eat away from home, you can teach them how to eat right by being a role model for them.

To meet a child's high-energy needs, snacks should be included in a nutritious diet. The kid-pleasing recipes in this chapter are snacks you can feel good about serving to your child.

Note: Children younger than 2 should not be put on a low-fat diet. Consult your pediatrician or family physician for further guidance.

■ STARCH/BREAD   ■ MEAT   ■ VEGETABLE   ■ FRUIT   ■ MILK   ■ FAT

On left (from left): *Peach Smoothie, page 104;*
Chocolate-Banana Shake, page 105

PEACH SMOOTHIE

MAKES 4 SERVINGS   PREP: 5 MINUTES

This frosty beverage (pictured on left on page 102) is a great way to add skim milk and fruit to your child's diet.

EXCHANGES

| ½ FRUIT |
| ½ MILK |

NUTRITION FACTS
PER 6-OUNCE SERVING

		Daily Values
Calories	70	3%
Total fat	0 g	0%
Saturated fat	0 g	0%
Cholesterol	1 mg	0%
Sodium	24 mg	1%
Carbohydrate	15 g	5%
Fiber	1 g	3%
Protein	2 g	

2 fresh medium peeled peaches or unpeeled nectarines, quartered, or ½ of a 16-ounce package frozen unsweetened peach slices
¾ cup skim milk
¼ cup frozen orange-pineapple juice concentrate, thawed
2 teaspoons sugar
1 teaspoon vanilla
1 cup ice cubes

1. If desired, set aside 4 peach or nectarine slices for garnish. In a blender container combine the remaining peaches or nectarines, the skim milk, juice concentrate, sugar, and vanilla. Cover and blend until smooth. Gradually add ice cubes through hole in blender lid, blending until smooth after each addition. If desired, garnish with reserved peach or nectarine slices.

EASY VEGGIE PIZZAS

MAKES 4 SERVINGS   PREP: 15 MINUTES   BAKE: 13 MINUTES

Kids always appreciate pizza. When you top these mini pizzas with vegetables, you'll know it's a snack that's tasty *and* nutritious.

EXCHANGES

| 2 STARCH |
| 1 VEGETABLE |

NUTRITION FACTS PER PIZZA

		Daily Values
Calories	198	9%
Total fat	3 g	5%
Saturated fat	1 g	4%
Cholesterol	4 mg	1%
Sodium	458 mg	19%
Carbohydrate	37 g	12%
Fiber	0 g	1%
Protein	9 g	

4 small wheat pita bread rounds or English muffin halves
Nonstick spray coating
¼ cup small broccoli flowerets, small cauliflower flowerets, chopped green sweet pepper, sliced fresh mushrooms, and/or finely chopped carrot
¼ cup pizza sauce
¼ cup shredded mozzarella cheese (1 ounce)

1. Place pitas or muffins on a baking sheet. Bake in a 400° oven for 5 minutes.

2. Meanwhile, spray an unheated small skillet with nonstick coating. Preheat over medium heat. Add vegetables and cook and stir until crisp-tender.

3. Spread pizza sauce on pitas or muffins; sprinkle with vegetables and cheese. Bake in a 400° oven for 8 to 10 minutes more or until light brown. Serve warm.

CHOCOLATE-BANANA SHAKE

MAKES 6 SERVINGS   PREP: 10 MINUTES

1½ cups vanilla fat-free yogurt
1¾ cups skim milk
1 small banana, cut into chunks
½ of a 4-serving-size package fat-free *instant* chocolate pudding mix (about 5 tablespoons)
4 fresh strawberries (optional)
Grated chocolate (optional)

1. In a blender container or food processor bowl, combine the yogurt, skim milk, banana, and pudding mix. Cover and blend or process until smooth. If desired, garnish with strawberries and grated chocolate.

Can't get your kids to drink milk? Bet you can with a glassful of this yummy shake (pictured on right on page 102).

EXCHANGES

| 1 FRUIT |
| ½ MILK |

NUTRITION FACTS PER 5⅓-OUNCE SERVING

		Daily Values
Calories	115	5%
Total fat	0 g	0%
Saturated fat	0 g	0%
Cholesterol	2 mg	0%
Sodium	189 mg	7%
Carbohydrate	24 g	7%
Fiber	0 g	1%
Protein	5 g	

PEANUT BUTTER AND OATMEAL COOKIES

MAKES ABOUT 36 COOKIES   PREP: 15 MINUTES   BAKE: 8 MINUTES PER BATCH

½ cup margarine or butter
½ cup reduced-fat or regular creamy peanut butter
⅓ cup granulated sugar
⅓ cup packed brown sugar
2 egg whites
½ teaspoon vanilla
1 cup all-purpose flour
½ teaspoon baking soda
1 cup quick-cooking rolled oats

1. In a large mixing bowl beat margarine or butter and peanut butter with an electric mixer on medium to high speed about 30 seconds or until margarine or butter is softened.

2. Add sugar and brown sugar to margarine mixture. Beat until thoroughly combined, scraping sides of bowl occasionally. Add egg whites and vanilla. Beat until well mixed. Add flour and baking soda. Beat on low speed until combined. Stir in oats.

3. Drop dough by rounded teaspoons 2 inches apart on an ungreased cookie sheet. Bake in a 375° oven about 8 minutes or until edges are golden. Transfer cookies to a wire rack. Cool completely.

Cookies are a kid's best friend. Pack your child's next lunch with these oat-filled treats.

EXCHANGES

| ½ STARCH |
| ½ FAT |

NUTRITION FACTS PER COOKIE

		Daily Values
Calories	78	3%
Total fat	4 g	6%
Saturated fat	1 g	4%
Cholesterol	0 mg	0%
Sodium	68 mg	2%
Carbohydrate	8 g	2%
Fiber	1 g	2%
Protein	2 g	

BANANA POPS

MAKES 6 SERVINGS   PREP: 15 MINUTES   FREEZE: 3 HOURS   STAND: 15 MINUTES

Crunchy, peanut-butter-coated, frozen bananas have all the ingredients to become a favorite snack for your children.

EXCHANGES
½ STARCH
½ FRUIT
½ FAT

NUTRITION FACTS PER SERVING

		Daily Values
Calories	97	4%
Total fat	3 g	5%
Saturated fat	1 g	3%
Cholesterol	0 mg	0%
Sodium	55 mg	2%
Carbohydrate	15 g	5%
Fiber	1 g	4%
Protein	3 g	

2 ripe medium bananas
6 wooden sticks
3 tablespoons skim milk
3 tablespoons reduced-fat or regular peanut butter
⅔ cup crushed almond crunch cereal, low-fat granola, or Grape Nuts cereal

1. Peel and cut each banana crosswise into 3 pieces. Insert a wooden stick into a cut end of each banana piece. Place on a baking sheet. Cover and freeze 1 hour or until bananas are firm.

2. Meanwhile, in a small mixing bowl gradually stir skim milk into peanut butter until smooth. Place cereal in a shallow dish or on a piece of waxed paper. Dip frozen bananas into peanut butter mixture to coat, letting excess drip off. Roll in cereal to coat.

3. Wrap each banana pop individually in plastic wrap. Return to the freezer. Freeze 2 hours more or until completely frozen. Let stand 15 minutes before eating.

TROPICAL FRUIT SHERBET POPS

MAKES 8 OR 12 SERVINGS   PREP: 15 MINUTES   FREEZE: 4 HOURS

Frozen pops made with real fruit are a parent's dream-come-true snack.

EXCHANGES
1 FRUIT

NUTRITION FACTS PER SERVING

		Daily Values
Calories	68	3%
Total fat	0 g	0%
Saturated fat	0 g	0%
Cholesterol	0 mg	0%
Sodium	42 mg	1%
Carbohydrate	16 g	5%
Fiber	1 g	3%
Protein	1 g	

½ cup boiling water
1 4-serving-size package sugar-free lemon-, mixed fruit-, or strawberry-flavored gelatin
1 15¼-ounce can crushed pineapple (juice pack)
2 medium bananas, peeled and cut into chunks
8 5- to 6-ounce or twelve 3-ounce paper cups
8 or 12 wooden sticks

1. In a 2-cup glass measure stir together boiling water and gelatin until gelatin dissolves. Pour into a blender container. Add *undrained* pineapple and banana chunks. Cover and blend until smooth.

2. Pour a scant ½ cup into each of the 5- to 6-ounce paper cups. (Or, pour a scant ⅓ cup into each of the 3-ounce paper cups.) Cover each cup with foil. Use the tip of a knife to make a small hole in the foil over each cup. Insert a wooden stick into the cup through the hole. Freeze 4 hours or until firm.

3. To serve, remove foil and tear off paper cups.

MENU SUGGESTIONS

These menus give you examples of how to use the recipes in this book and the Daily Meal Plans on page 13. For your personal meal plan, determine your calorie level (see pages 6 through 13), then pick a meal plan from page 13 that most closely fits your needs. Refer to the menus below and on page 108 as guides for choosing recipes and other foods based on your meal plan. For your convenience, we've included a blank meal plan on page 109 to record the exchanges you're allowed for a day. Photocopy the page, enter your personal meal plan, fold the sheet into fourths, and carry it with you to refer to during the day. Any recipe in this book can fit into your meals. Just keep track of the number of exchanges allowed in Your Meal Plan. As you eat a certain food or recipe, subtract the exchanges that you've used from your totals for the day.

1,200-Calorie Menu

BREAKFAST

Whole Wheat Pumpkin Muffins, page 20
(*1 Starch, ½ Fat*)

Margarine or butter, 1 teaspoon (*1 Fat*)

Fruit, such as 1¼ cups whole strawberries or ½ cup canned pineapple (*1 Fruit*)

Milk, 1 cup (*1 Milk*)

LUNCH

Pinto Bean and Cheese Burritos, page 67
(*2 Starch, 1 Medium-Fat Meat, ½ Vegetable*)

Rice, ⅓ cup cooked (*1 Starch*)

Tomato, ½ cup chopped (*½ Vegetable*)

Iced tea (*Free*)

Strawberry Frozen Dessert, page 86
(*1 Fruit, ½ Milk*)

SNACK

Assorted vegetable dippers, 1 cup
(*1 Vegetable*)

Roasted Red Pepper Dip, page 100 (*Free*)

DINNER

Salmon with Fruit Salsa, page 57
(*2 Lean Meat, ½ Fruit*)

Steamed green beans, ½ cup (*1 Vegetable*)

Small dinner roll (*1 Starch*)

Margarine or butter, 1 teaspoon (*1 Fat*)

DESSERT OR SNACK

Cherry Brownies, page 91 (*1 Starch, ½ Fat*)

Milk, ½ cup (*1 Milk*)

1,500-Calorie Menu

BREAKFAST

Streusel Coffee Cake, page 23
(*2 Starch, ½ Fruit, 1 Fat*)

Fruit, such as 1 medium peach, sliced
(*1 Fruit*)

Milk, 1 cup (*1 Milk*)

Hot coffee or tea (*Free*)

LUNCH

Hot Turkey Sub Sandwich, page 39
(*2 Starch, 1½ Lean Meat, 1 Vegetable, ½ Fat*)

Vegetable Pasta Salad, page 73
(*1 Starch, 1 Vegetable, 1 Fat*)

Diet soft drink (*Free*)

DESSERT OR SNACK

Oatmeal-Applesauce Cake, page 87
(*1 Starch, 1 Fruit, ½ Fat*)

Milk, 1 cup (*1 Milk*)

DINNER

Chutney-Sauced Chicken, page 33
(*2½ Very Lean Meat, 1 Fruit*)

Steamed broccoli, ½ cup (*1 Vegetable*)

Yogurt Drop Biscuits, page 78
(*1 Starch, ½ Fat*)

Margarine or butter, 1 teaspoon (*1 Fat*)

SNACK

Curried Snack Mix, page 100 (*1 Starch*)

1,800-Calorie Menu

BREAKFAST

"Sausage" Breakfast Casserole, page 25
   (*1 Starch, 1 Lean Meat, ½ Milk*)

Melon, 1 cup cubed (*1 Fruit*)

Apple juice, ½ cup (*1 Fruit*)

Hot coffee or tea (*Free*)

LUNCH

Honey Ham Salad, page 51
   (*1 Lean Meat, 2 Vegetable, ½ Fruit*)

Small dinner roll (*1 Starch*)

Margarine or butter, 2 teaspoons (*2 Fat*)

Milk, 1 cup (*1 Milk*)

Lemon Cake, page 90 (*2 Starch, ½ Fat*)

SNACK

Apple, 1 small (*1 Fruit*)

DINNER

Hearty Beef Stew, page 44
   (*1½ Starch, 2 Lean Meat, 2 Vegetable*)

Pepper Corn Bread, page 78 (*2 Starch*)

Margarine or butter, 2 teaspoons (*2 Fat*)

Milk (*1 Milk*)

SNACK

Pudding, regular, ½ cup (*2 Starch*)

Banana, 1 small (*1 Fruit*)

2,000-Calorie Menu

BREAKFAST

Breakfast Crepes, page 28
   (*½ Starch, 1 Fruit, ½ Milk, ½ Fat*)

Canadian bacon or sausage (with 3 grams fat
   or less), 1 ounce (*1 Lean Meat*)

Cranberry juice cocktail, reduced-calorie,
   ⅓ cup (*1 Fruit*)

LUNCH

Creamy Fish Chowder, page 59
   (*1½ Lean Meat, 2 Vegetable, ½ Milk*)

Bagel, 1 (*2 Starch*)

Reduced-fat cream cheese, 2 tablespoons
   (*1 Fat*)

Mixed greens salad, 1 cup (*1 Vegetable*)

Salad dressing, 2 tablespoons (*2 Fat*)

Mint-Chocolate Chip Ice Milk, page 85
   (*½ Starch, ½ Milk*)

SNACK

Fat-free granola bar, 1 bar (*2 Starch*)

Milk, 1 cup (*1 Milk*)

Nectarine, 1 small (*1 Fruit*)

DINNER

Tomato-Stuffed Chicken Rolls, page 35
   (*2½ Very Lean Meat, ½ Vegetable*)

Pasta, 1 cup (*2 Starch*)

Olive oil, 1 teaspoon (*1 Fat*)

Peas, ½ cup (*1 Starch*)

Breadsticks, two 4-inch-long sticks
   (*1 Starch*)

Margarine or butter, 2 teaspoons (*2 Fat*)

Fruit juice bar (*1 Fruit*)

SNACK

Curried Snack Mix, page 100 (*1 Starch*)

Orange, 1 small (*1 Fruit*)

YOUR MEAL PLAN

After choosing the calorie level based on your own needs (see the introduction beginning on page 4), pick a Daily Meal Plan from page 13 and record your own personal exchange totals on a photocopy of this page. Write the number of exchanges from each food group into the spaces provided on the table below.

Fold the photocopy on the dotted lines and carry it with you to work and restaurants. (This page also includes a simplified breakdown of the Exchange Lists.)

As you lose weight, the number of calories you can eat will change. Simply photocopy this page again and write in your new meal plan. Remember: You can move your exchanges to any meal or snack throughout the day. Just keep the total number consumed consistent to stay within your calorie range.

CALORIES ____

	Breakfast	Lunch	Snack	Dinner	Snack
STARCH (__)					
MEAT (__)					
VEGETABLE (__)					
FRUIT (__)					
MILK (Skim)(__)					
FAT (__)					

EXCHANGES

Use these abbreviated lists as general guides to serving amounts (see full Exchange Lists located on the inside covers of front and back of book):

ONE STARCH EXCHANGE IS:

1 ounce of a bread product, such as 1 slice of bread
½ cup cooked cereal, grain, pasta, or starchy vegetable such as corn
¾ to 1 ounce of most snack foods

ONE MEAT EXCHANGE IS:

1 ounce cooked meat, poultry, or fish
1 ounce cheese
1 egg
½ cup cooked dried beans, peas, lentils
2 tablespoons peanut butter
3 slices bacon

ONE VEGETABLE EXCHANGE IS:

1 cup raw vegetables such as lettuce, spinach, or broccoli flowerets
½ cup cooked vegetables or vegetable juice

ONE FRUIT EXCHANGE IS:

1 small to medium piece of fresh fruit such as an apple or orange
½ cup canned or fresh fruit or fruit juice
¼ cup dried fruit

ONE MILK EXCHANGE IS:

1 cup milk
1 cup yogurt

ONE FAT EXCHANGE IS:

1 teaspoon vegetable oil, regular margarine, butter, or mayonnaise
1 tablespoon regular salad dressing
6 almonds or cashews, or 4 pecan or walnut halves
2 teaspoons peanut butter
1 slice bacon

COMBINATION FOODS

ENTRÉES

1 cup tuna noodle casserole, lasagna, spaghetti with meatballs, chili with beans, macaroni and cheese
Count as 2 Starch, 2 Medium-Fat Meat

¼ of a 10-inch pizza with meat topping, thin crust
Count as 2 Starch, 1 Medium-Fat Meat, 4 Fat

FROZEN ENTRÉES

8 ounces turkey with gravy, mashed potato, dressing
Count as 2 Starch, 2 Medium-Fat Meat, 2 Fat

8-ounce entrée with less than 300 calories
Count as 2 Starch, 3 Lean Meat

SOUPS

½ cup split pea (made with water)
1 cup tomato (made with water)
1 cup vegetable beef, chicken noodle, or other broth-type
Count as 1 Starch

INDEX

Page numbers in boldface type indicate a photograph.

METRIC COOKING HINTS

By making a few conversions, cooks in Australia, Canada, and the United Kingdom can use the recipes in *Better Homes and Gardens® Eat & Stay Slim* with confidence. The charts on this page provide a guide for converting measurements from the U.S. customary system, which is used throughout this book, to the imperial and metric systems. There also is a conversion table for oven temperatures to accommodate the differences in oven calibrations.

Product Differences: Most of the ingredients called for in the recipes in this book are available in English-speaking countries. However, some are known by different names. Here are some common American ingredients and their possible counterparts:
■ Sugar is granulated or castor sugar.
■ Powdered sugar is icing sugar.
■ All-purpose flour is plain household flour or white flour. When self-rising flour is used in place of all-purpose flour in a recipe that calls for leavening, omit the leavening agent (baking soda or baking powder) and salt.
■ Light corn syrup is golden syrup.
■ Cornstarch is cornflour.
■ Baking soda is bicarbonate of soda.
■ Vanilla is vanilla essence.
■ Green, red, and yellow sweet peppers are capsicums.
■ Sultanas are golden raisins.

Volume and Weight: Americans traditionally use cup measures for liquid and solid ingredients. The chart at top right shows the approximate imperial and metric equivalents. If you are accustomed to weighing solid ingredients, the following approximate equivalents will be helpful.
■ 1 cup butter, castor sugar, or rice = 8 ounces = about 250 grams
■ 1 cup flour = 4 ounces = about 125 grams
■ 1 cup icing sugar = 5 ounces = about 150 grams
Spoon measures are used for smaller amounts of ingredients. Although the size of the tablespoon varies slightly in different countries, for practical purposes and for recipes in this book, a straight substitution is all that's necessary.
Measurements made using cups or spoons always should be level unless stated otherwise.

EQUIVALENTS: U.S. = AUSTRALIA/U.K.

⅛ teaspoon = 0.5 millilitre
¼ teaspoon = 1 millilitre
½ teaspoon = 2 millilitres
1 teaspoon = 5 millilitres
1 tablespoon = 1 tablespoon
¼ cup = 2 tablespoons = 2 fluid ounces = 60 millilitres
⅓ cup = ¼ cup = 3 fluid ounces = 90 millilitres
½ cup = ⅓ cup = 4 fluid ounces = 120 millilitres
⅔ cup = ½ cup = 5 fluid ounces = 150 millilitres
¾ cup = ⅔ cup = 6 fluid ounces = 180 millilitres
1 cup = ¾ cup = 8 fluid ounces = 240 millilitres
1¼ cups = 1 cup
2 cups = 1 pint
1 quart = 1 litre
½ inch = 1.27 centimetres
1 inch = 2.54 centimetres

BAKING PAN SIZES

American	Metric
8×1½-inch round baking pan	20×4-centimetre cake tin
9×1½-inch round baking pan	23×3.5-centimetre cake tin
11×7×1½-inch baking pan	28×18×4-centimetre baking tin
13×9×2-inch baking pan	30×20×3-centimetre baking tin
2-quart rectangular baking dish	30×20×3-centimetre baking tin
15×10×1-inch baking pan	30×25×2-centimetre baking tin (Swiss roll tin)
9-inch pie plate	22×4- or 23×4-centimetre pie plate
7- or 8-inch springform pan	18- or 20-centimetre springform or loose-bottom cake tin
9×5×3-inch loaf pan	23×13×7-centimetre or 2-pound narrow loaf tin or paté tin
1½-quart casserole	1.5-litre casserole
2-quart casserole	2-litre casserole

OVEN TEMPERATURE EQUIVALENTS

Fahrenheit Setting	Celsius Setting*	Gas Setting
300°F	150°C	Gas Mark 2 (slow)
325°F	160°C	Gas Mark 3 (moderately slow)
350°F	180°C	Gas Mark 4 (moderate)
375°F	190°C	Gas Mark 5 (moderately hot)
400°F	200°C	Gas Mark 6 (hot)
425°F	220°C	Gas Mark 7
450°F	230°C	Gas Mark 8 (very hot)
Broil		Grill

* Electric and gas ovens may be calibrated using Celsius. However, for an electric oven, increase the Celsius setting 10° to 20° when cooking above 160°C. For convection or forced-air ovens (gas or electric), lower the temperature setting 10°C when cooking at all heat levels.

The Exchange Lists are based on a meal planning system designed by the American Diabetes Association and The American Dietetic Association. While designed primarily for those with diabetes, the exchanges are based on principles of good nutrition that apply to everyone.

COMBINATION FOODS

Many of the foods we eat are combined in mixtures. These combinations of foods may not fit into any one exchange list. Below is a list of exchanges for some typical combination foods to help you fit combination foods into your meal plan. Ask your dietitian to help you determine exchanges for any other combination foods you'd like to include in your meal plan.

Food	Serving size	Exchanges per serving
Entrées		
Tuna noodle casserole, chili with beans, lasagna, macaroni and cheese, spaghetti with meatballs	1 cup (8 oz.)	2 Starch, 2 Medium-Fat Meat
Chow mein (without noodles or rice)	2 cups (16 oz.)	1 Starch, 2 Lean Meat
Pizza, cheese, thin crust*	1/4 of 10" (5 oz.)	2 Starch, 2 Medium-Fat Meat, 1 Fat
Pizza, meat topping, thin crust* (5 oz.)	1/4 of 10"	2 Starch, 2 Medium-Fat Meat, 2 Fat

Food	Serving size	Exchanges per serving
Frozen entrées		
Entrée with less than 300 calories	1 (8 oz.)	2 Starch, 3 Lean Meat
Salisbury steak with gravy, mashed potato*	1 (11 oz.)	2 Starch, 3 Medium-Fat Meat, 3–4 Fat
Turkey with gravy, mashed potato, dressing*	1 (11 oz.)	2 Starch, 2 Medium-Fat Meat, 2 Fat
Potpie*	1 (7 oz.)	2 Starch, 1 Medium-Fat Meat, 4 Fat

Food	Serving Size	Exchanges per Serving
Soups		
Bean*	1 cup (8 oz.)	1 Starch, 1 Very Lean Meat
Cream* (made with water)	1 cup	1 Starch, 1 Fat
Split pea* (made with water)	½ cup (4 oz.)	1 Starch
Tomato* (made with water)	1 cup	1 Starch
Vegetable beef, chicken noodle or other broth-type*	1 cup	1 Starch

* = 400 mg or more sodium per exchange

SPECIAL FOODS

Below is a list of exchanges for some typical foods you may occasionally enjoy eating. Use these foods in moderation.

Food	Serving size	Exchanges per serving
Angel food cake, unfrosted	1/12th cake	2 Starch
Brownie, small unfrosted	2" square	1 Starch, 1 Fat
Cake, frosted	2" square	2 Starch, 1 Fat
Cake, unfrosted	2" square	1 Starch, 1 Fat
Cookie, Fat-free	2 small	1 Starch
Cookie or sandwich cookie with cream filling	2 small	1 Starch, 1 Fat
Cranberry sauce, jellied	¼ cup	2 Fruit
Cupcake frosted	1 small	2 Starch, 1 Fat
Doughnut, glazed	3¾" across	2 Starch, 2 Fat
Doughnut, plain cake	1 medium (1½ oz.)	1½ Starch, 2 Fat
Fruit juice bars, frozen, 100% juice	1 bar (3 oz.)	1 Fruit

Food	Serving size	Exchanges per serving
Fruit snacks, chewy (pureed fruit concentrate)	1 roll (¾ oz.)	1 Fruit
Fruit spreads, 100% fruit	1 Tbsp.	1 Fruit
Gelatin, regular	½ cup	1 Starch
Gingersnaps	3	1 Starch
Granola bar	1 bar	1 Starch, 1 Fat
Granola bar, fat-free	1 bar	2 Starch
Ice cream	½ cup	1 Starch, 2 Fat
Ice cream, fat-free, no sugar added	½ cup	1 Starch
Ice cream, light	½ cup	1 Starch
Jam or jelly, regular	1 Tbsp.	1 Fruit
Milk, chocolate, whole	1 cup	2 Starch, 1 Fat
Pie, fruit, 2 crusts	1/6 pie	2 Starch, 1 Fruit, 2 Fat
Pie, pumpkin or custard	1/8 pie	1 Starch, 2 Fat
Potato chips	12–18 (1 oz.)	1 Starch, 2 Fat

Food	Serving size	Exchanges per serving
Pudding, regular (made with low-fat milk)	½ cup	2 Starch
Pudding, sugar-free (made with low-fat milk)	½ cup	1 Starch
Salad dressing, fat-free*	¼ cup	1 Starch
Sherbet, sorbet	½ cup	2 Starch
Spaghetti or pasta sauce, canned*	½ cup	1 Starch, 1 Fat
Sweet roll or Danish	1 (2½ oz.)	2½ Starch, 2 Fat
Syrup, light	2 Tbsp.	1 Starch
Syrup, regular	1 Tbsp.	1 Starch
Tortilla chips	6–12 (1 oz.)	1 Starch, 2 Fat
Vanilla wafers	5	1 Starch, 1 Fat
Yogurt, frozen, fat-free, no sugar added	½ cup	1 Fruit
Yogurt, frozen, low-fat, fat-free	⅓ cup	1 Fruit, 0–1 Fat
Yogurt, low-fat with fruit	1 cup	3 Fruit, 0–1 Fat

* = 400 mg or more sodium per exchange